GRE Vocab Capacity

Powerful Memory Tricks and Mnemonics to Widen your Lexicon

Now with more than 1000 mnemonics!

By

Brian McElroy

and

Vince Kotchian

Contents

Introduction

Brian McElroy (Harvard, '02) and Vince Kotchian (Boston College, '97), two of San Diego's most sought after test-prep tutors, provide a series of clever, unconventional, and funny memory devices aimed toward helping you to improve your vocabulary and remember words long-term so that you don't ever forget their meanings. Brian and Vince have both taken the GRE and, combined, have been tutoring the test for over 20 years. They have analyzed all available official GRE tests to select the words that appear in this book.

The vocabulary words in this book are best suited for students at a 9th-grade level or above. The words in this edition are specifically targeted toward the GRE exam, but they are also helpful for students who are preparing for other standardized tests such as the SAT, ACT, ISEE, SSAT, GMAT, LSAT or MCAT, or anyone at any age who simply wants to improve his/her knowledge of English vocabulary.

Disclaimer: a few of the mnemonics might not be appropriate for kids – some contain adult language or situations.

Why This Book Is Different

If you're studying for the GRE, SAT, or for any other standardized test that measures your vocabulary, you may be feeling a little bit anxious – especially if you've taken a practice test and encountered words you didn't know (or maybe never even saw before)! Whether you have seven days or seven months to prepare for the test, you're going to want to boost your vocabulary. But it's not that simple –

you've got to *remember* the words you learn. And on many GRE text completion and sentence equivalence questions, getting the right answer comes down to knowing the precise definition of the words.

You could make vocabulary flashcards. You could look up words you don't know. You could read a book with lots of big words. But unless you give your brain a way to hold on to the words you learn, it will probably have a harder time remembering them when they appear on the test. That's the problem with most vocabulary books: the definitions and sentences in the books aren't especially memorable.

That's where this book is different. We've not only clearly defined the words but we've also created sentences designed to help you remember the words through a variety of associations - using mnemonics.

Mnemonic Examples

A mnemonic is just a memory device. It works by creating a link in your brain to something else, so that recall of one thing helps recall of the other. This can be done in many ways – but the strongest links are through senses, emotions, rhymes, and patterns.

Consider this example:

Quash (verb): to completely stop from happening.

Think: SQUASH.

The best way to QUASH an invasion of ants in your kitchen is simple: SQUASH them.

Now your brain has a link from the word **quash** (which it may not have known) to the word **squash** (which it probably knows). Both words sound and look the same, so it's easy to create a visual and aural link. If you picture someone squashing ants (and maybe get grossed out), you also have another visual link and an emotional link.

Here's another example:

Eschew (verb): to avoid.

Think: AH-CHOO!

ESCHEW people who say "AH-CHOO!" unless you want to catch their colds.

The word **eschew** sounds similar to a sneeze (**ah-choo!**), so your brain will now link the two sounds. If you picture yourself avoiding someone who is about to sneeze in your face, even better! Again, the more connections you make in your brain to the new word, the easier it will be for you to recall it.

Word Root Examples

Word roots are parts of words that often mean the same thing. For example, the root CHRON pretty much always has something to do with time: syn**chron**ize, **chron**ological, etc. So knowing what word roots mean can be useful in helping you learn words. They can also provide a hint for the meaning of words that you don't know.

However, English is a funny language, and roots don't always have the same meaning - it can depend on what word they're in. So what you *shouldn't* expect from roots is that they'll be reliable to help you determine the definition of a word you don't know. If you're preparing for a standardized test like the GRE or SAT, keep in mind that knowing your word roots is not a substitute for knowing the actual definitions of words.

We've included an appendix with this book that lists many common word roots along with their usual definitions, and an easy example word that uses the root. For example:

CHRON: time.

Think: **CHRON**ological: arranged in order of time.

We recommend learning all the word roots if you have time. They'll be helpful in broadening your lexicon.

Tip: the more letters you can match from the beginning of a word you know to a word you don't know, the more likely it is they have similar meanings. Matching five or more letters is a good benchmark.

For example, if you know that **pacifist** has to do with being peaceful, you'd be right in guessing that **pacific** has a similar meaning since they both start with **pacifi**.

However, matching only a few letters is much less reliable. For example, the words **garrulous** and **garish** don't have similar meanings.

How To Use This Book

One tool we recommend is periodic review. For example, select the first five words in the book that you can't define, and read their entries. Try to visualize an image that makes you react emotionally as you think about each mnemonic. The next day you study, pick five new words, and do the same. Then, go back to the first day's words and see if you remember their definitions. Put one star next to those you remember. On the third day of studying, pick five new words as usual, and review all ten previous words. Those you know get a star; those you still know (from the first day) get another star. Repeat this process. Once a word gets three stars, stop reviewing it – you've probably learned it for good.

Go back to your three-star words once a month or so. If you've forgotten any, take away their stars and add them to the process as if they're new.

It's often useful to hear the correct pronunciations of words you don't know. Try http://www.forvo.com/ or a similar site that has audio recordings of words.

It may be helpful to learn all the word roots first and then begin learning words you don't know, looking for instances of the roots to help you learn the new words.

For troublesome words - or for any word you want to be sure of - we recommend writing down the word's definition *in your own words*, then making up your own sentence using the word. Until you can explain something in your own words, you probably don't fully understand it, and your own definitions and sentences will often be more memorable than ours. Some people go straight to the most bizarre looking words in the book, but don't overlook the words that you "kind of" know but can't easily define. That goes for words outside this book, too. If you can't easily define a word you see in the newspaper, for instance, look it up!

Tip: for words that just won't stick in your brain, try associating a movement with the word. Making a specific gesture with your body every time you study the word will provide an additional connection in your memory.

One last tip: **use it or lose it**! The more you can work your new vocabulary into your daily speech and writing, the more you'll remember it. You might sound nerdy, but it's worth it.

We've also included a number next to each word indicating its relative difficulty, using the following scale:

1. Basic word that could appear on any level of an exam.

2. More challenging words, but those that commonly appear on tests.

3. Difficult words that appear somewhat more rarely.

4. Uncommon words (that probably won't appear on a test but that might be useful to know).

Our hope is that this book not only helps you improve your vocabulary, but also inspires you to start creating your own mnemonics!

- Brian and Vince

P.S. - We always appreciate reviews of *GRE Vocab Capacity* on Amazon.com, and we welcome any feedback or suggestions that you might have. Seriously. Feel free to send us an email!

We're also available for private tutoring of the SAT, ACT, GRE, GMAT, and ISEE either in person (in San Diego) or online (via Skype).

mcelroy@post.harvard.edu (Brian McElroy)
vkotchian@gmail.com (Vince Kotchian)
www.McElroyTutoring.com

The Mnemonics

Abase (verb): to humiliate or degrade. 2

Think: Give up A BASE.

When you're making out with someone, if you give up A BASE too quickly, then you just ABASE yourself.

Abashed (adjective): embarrassed. 2

Think: BASHFUL the dwarf.

When Snow White kisses him, BASHFUL gets so ABASHED that he blushes.

Abate (verb): to reduce. 2

Think: REBATE.

It may be annoying to have to mail it in, but the REBATE on the new cell phone will ABATE its cost.

Aberration (noun): an exception or departure from the norm. 2

Think: A BARE ASIAN.

Seeing A BARE ASIAN would be an ABERRATION – Asians usually wear clothes.

Abeyance (noun): temporary inactivity; suspension. 3

Think: "OBEY" ENDS. *hiatus*

When our lieutenant's command to OBEY ENDS, our work plans are held in ABEYANCE because we're lazy.

Abhors (verb): hates. 2

Think: AB-WHORE.

Daria ABHORS the tube-top-wearing blonde who stole her boyfriend and refers to her as an "AB-WHORE".

Abject (adjective): miserable; wretched; hopeless. 2

Think: REJECTS.

If she REJECTS my marriage proposal, I'll be ABJECT, with nothing to live for.

Abnegate (verb): to give up something; to deny oneself something. 3 *Abdicate*

Think: ABS NEGATED.

If you ABNEGATE food, the fat covering your ABS will get NEGATED.

Abomination (noun): something awful. 2

Think: BOMB A NATION.

It is an ABOMINATION to BOMB a NATION.

Aboriginal (adjective): existing since the beginning. 3

Think: ORIGINAL.

In Australia, the ORIGINAL natives are the Aborigines - they are ABORIGINAL since they were its first inhabitants.

Abort (verb): to end prematurely. 1

Think: ABORTION.

An ABORTION can ABORT a pregnancy.

Abound (verb): to be numerous. 2

Think: ABUNDANT.

Kangaroos ABOUND in Australia; they're ABUNDANT, bouncing around wherever you look.

Abridge (verb): to shorten. 1

Think: A BRIDGE.

A BRIDGE would ABRIDGE my commute, which involves driving around the canyon.

Abrogate (verb): to get rid of; to abolish. 3

Think: A BROKEN GATE.

After the elephant sat on it

After my 120 lb. mastiff decided to ABROGATE the barrier to the kitchen and eat from the garbage, we were left with A BROKEN GATE.

Abscission (noun): the shedding of leaves, flowers, or fruits. 3 inscission

Think: SCISSORS.

Instead of waiting for the grapes to drop off of the vines, speed up the ABSCISSION by getting out there with a pair of SCISSORS.

trimming

Absolve (verb): to free from guilt; to forgive. 2

Think: DISSOLVE.

Catholics believe that confessing to a priest will DISSOLVE their guilt and ABSOLVE them from sin.

Abstemious (adjective): sparing or moderate. 3

parsemonious [handwritten]

Think: ABSTINENCE.

The health teacher knew that if he told students to be
ABSTEMIOUS, some of them would still get pregnant, so
he urged them to practice ABSTINENCE.

Abstruse (adjective): hard to comprehend. 2

obtuse [handwritten]

Think: ABSTRACT and CONFUSING.

The ABSTRACT strudel directions will CONFUSE the
new cook because they are ABSTRUSE.

Abysmal (adjective): awful. 2

Think: PEPTO-BISMOL.

When I had food poisoning, my stomach felt so
ABYSMAL that I had to drink a bottle of PEPTO-
BISMOL.

Accede (verb): to express approval for; to give into. 2

accept [handwritten]

Think: AGREED.

Since we all ACCEDE to the plan to seed the garden, it
looks like we're AGREED.

Acerbic (adjective): harsh; biting. 2

Think: ACIDIC.

On American Idol, Simon Cowell's criticism was ACERBIC to the point of being ACIDIC.

Acidulous (adjective): somewhat harsh. 3

Think: ACID-ISH.

I like Sour Patch Kids because their ACIDULOUS taste is ACID-ISH without being too painful.

Acquisitive (adjective): eager to acquire and possess; greedy. 3

aquire

Think: A SQUID VISITED.

An ACQUISITIVE SQUID VISITED my house and wrapped his arms around all of my valuable Chinese porcelain.

Acrimonious (adjective): bitter. 2   *Acrid*

Think: A CRIME ON US.

Committing A CRIME ON US makes us ACRIMONIOUS.

Acumen (noun): insightfulness. 2

Think: ACCURATE MEN.

In business, ACCURATE MEN usually have ACUMEN.

Adamant (adjective): stubborn; unyielding. 2

Think: ADAM…DAMN IT!

God was ADAMANT that ADAM not return to the Garden of Eden: "I said no, DAMN IT!"

Adept (adjective): very skilled. 1

Think: ADAPT.

Mountain lions can ADAPT to almost any climate and environment; they're ADEPT at survival.

Admonished (verb): warned to do what's best. 2

Think: ADD MONISTAT.

"ADD MONISTAT to your body if you're suffering from a vaginal yeast infection," the ad ADMONISHED.

Adorned (adjective): decorated. 2

Think: ADD ORNAMENTS.

If you adore Christmas, then you probably enjoy ADORNING your home by ADDING ORNAMENTS to your tree.

Adroit (adjective): skillful. 2

Think: A DROID.

A DROID is an ADROIT cell phone since it can do so much.

Adulation (noun): excessive admiration. 3

Jubilation

Think: ADULT ADORATION.

The grown ADULT'S ADORATION of role-playing video games could only be called ADULATION.

Adulterate (verb): to corrupt; to make impure. 2

Think: ADULTERY.

In The Bible, God said, "Thou shalt not commit ADULTERY" because an affair will ADULTERATE a marriage.

Aegis (noun): protection. 3

Think: EGG US!

Go ahead, try to EGG US - our house has the AEGIS of the police, since my dad's a cop.

Aesthetic (adjective): relating to beauty. 1

Think: ATHLETIC body.

If you're ATHLETIC, then you're likely to have a body that is AESTHETICally pleasing.

Affable (adjective): friendly. 2

Think: LAUGHABLE.

Since they want tourists to feed them, zoo GIRAFFES are so AFFABLE that it's LAUGHABLE.

Affectation (noun): an artificial way of behaving. 2

Think: A FAKE FICTION.

Madonna's phony English accent is an AFFECTATION; it is A FAKE FICTION.

Aggrandized (verb): made greater; enhanced. 2

Think: A GRAND-SIZED.

I AGGRANDIZED my social status by throwing a lavish party - it gave me A GRAND-SIZED reputation.

Aghast (adjective): struck by fear or amazement. 2

Think: A GHOST.

I was AGHAST when I looked in the mirror and saw A GHOST standing next to me.

Algorithm (noun): a mathematical formula or procedure. 2

Think: AL GORE'S RHYTHM.

It's an inconvenient truth that, on the dance floor, AL GORE'S RHYTHM is as dull and predictable as a computer ALGORITHM.

Alleviate (verb): to soothe or lessen the severity of. 2

Think: ALEVE.

Allison's headache was so bad that she took four ALEVE pills to ALLEVIATE the pain.

Altruistic (adjective): unselfish concern for others. 2

Think: ALWAYS TRUE STICK.

My wingman is ALTRUISTIC: he's ALWAYS TRUE to me and will STICK by my side when I hit on chicks - even if he's not interested in any of them.

Amalgamate (verb): unify; join parts into a whole. 2

Think: GUM.

After breaking the vase, MALCOLM used GUM to AMALGAMATE the pieces back together.

Ameliorated (verb): made better. 2

Think: EMILIO RATED.

EMILIO RATED my pasta as a 10 out of 10, which AMELIORATED my fear that I had ruined it.

Amenable (adjective): willing; cooperative. 2

Think: AMEN-ABLE.

After she shouted, "AMEN!" I was able to tell that she was AMENABLE to my plan.

Amicable (adjective): friendly. 2

Think: HAMMOCK-ABLE.

When AMY reminded me that her HAMMOCK was ABLE to hold two people, I knew that she was AMICABLE.

Amortize (verb): to gradually pay off or reduce. 3

Think: A MORTGAGE.

AMOrtize the mortgage.

Unless you have a ton of money, when you buy a house, you probably AMORTIZE the loan with A MORTGAGE.

Anachronism (noun): something belonging to a different time period. 2

Think: INACCURATE CHRONOLOGY.

The movie has something INACCURATE about its CHRONOLOGY: a caveman wearing a watch - a huge ANACHRONISM.

Anathema (noun): something hated; a curse. 2

Think: A NASTY ENEMA.

If a patient is constipated, then A NASTY ENEMA may follow, which can be ANATHEMA for the nurse.

Anile (adjective): senile. 4

Think: SENILE.

I knew my Aunt Ann was ANILE to the point of being SENILE when she asked to go swimming in the Nile.

Animosity (noun): hatred; hostility. 1

Think: ENEMY CITY.

During the war, I accidentally parachuted into the ENEMY CITY and was met with ANIMOSITY.

Annotation (noun): a comment or note on a literary work. 2

Think: A NOTATION.

There are lots of ANNOTATIONS in my copy of *Hamlet*; I made A NOTATION every time I needed to define an unfamiliar term.

Anodyne (noun): a pain-reliever. 4

Think: AM NOT DYING.

I have the flu, but my doctor-prescribed ANODYNE finally has made me feel like I AM NOT DYING.

Anomaly (noun): something unusual. 2

Think: ABNORMALLY KNOBBY KNEE.

I have an ABNORMALLY KNOBBY KNEE; my doctor tells me it's an ANOMALY.

Antedate (verb): to come before. 3

Think: AUNTIE ANTE- (before) DATE.

Chances are that your AUNTIE has a birth DATE that ANTEDATES yours.

Antediluvian (adjective): ancient; primitive. 3

[handwritten: Fresno 79 PCL]

Think: ANTI-DILDO-LOVIN'.

Only someone with ANTEDILUVIAN views on sex would be ANTI-DILDO-LOVIN'.

Antipode (noun): the exact opposite. 3

Think: ANTI-POLE.

The North POLE is the ANTIPODE to the South POLE - you might say they're "ANTI-POLES."

Antithesis (noun): opposite. 2

Think: ANTI-THESIS.

You got a "D" on your essay because your examples argued for the ANTITHESIS of your introduction's THESIS.

Apace (adverb): quickly. 3

Think: KEEP PACE.

The Indy 500 racer's pit crew changed his tires APACE so he could KEEP PACE with the leaders.

Apartheid (noun): the policy of separating groups based on race. 2

Think: APART TO HIDE.

In South Africa, APARTHEID kept blacks APART TO HIDE them from racist whites.

Aplomb (noun): confidence. 2

Think: The BOMB.

If you have APLOMB, you think you're the BOMB.

Apocryphal (adjective): of doubtful truthfulness. 3

Think: APOCALYPSE predictions.

The prediction that the APOCALYPSE would happen in 2012 turned out to be APOCRYPHAL.

Apoplectic (adjective): enraged. 2

Think: APU EPILEPTIC.

In the Simpsons, when Nelson robbed his Quickie Mart, Apu shook with APOPLECTIC rage as if he was having an EPILEPTIC seizure.

Apothegm (noun): a short, wise remark. 3

Think: POCKET THE GEM.

Fortune from cookie in pocket

"POCKET THE GEM!" is a good APOTHEGM to remember if you're training to be a jewelry store robber.

Apotheosis (noun): a perfect example. 3

Think: A POTENT THESIS.

My professor said he gave me only A in the class because my paper was the APOTHEOSIS of a persuasive essay: it had A POTENT THESIS.

Appease (verb): to soothe, satisfy or pacify. 1

Think: PLEASE with PEAS.

I APPEASE and PLEASE my baby daughter by hiding her PEAS inside of her mashed potatoes.

Apportion (verb): to divide and distribute. 2

Think: A PORTION.

If you want A PORTION of lunch, go ask the lunch lady - she APPORTIONS it to everyone.

Apposite (adjective): appropriate. 3

Think: A POSITIVE SITE.

Wikipedia is A POSITIVE SITE because it's APPOSITE for all kinds of research.

Approbation (noun): approval; praise. 2

approval.

Think: APPROVE PROBATION.

Maybe the best APPROBATION I ever received was when the judge finally APPROVED me for PROBATION.

Apropos (adjective): relevant. 2

Think: APPROPRIATE.

It's APROPOS and APPROPRIATE that we're talking about POSING because I was just discovered and contracted to be a model!

Arch (adjective): sassy. 2

Think: ARCHED EYEBROW.

Her playful, ARCH comment made me ARCH my eyebrow.

Archaic (adjective): no longer current; outdated. 1

Think: ARCH AGE.

I knew you time-traveled here from the Roman Empire because your ARCHAIC expressions sound like you're from the ARCH AGE.

Arduous (adjective): strenuous; difficult. 2

Think: HARD FOR US.

Clearing out that hoarder's house is ARDUOUS; it's HARD FOR US because he kept every piece of junk mail he ever received.

Arid (adjective): very dry. 1

Think: ARRID Extra Dry.

"Get a little closer; don't be shy! Get a little closer, with ARRID Extra Dry deodorant (which keeps your armpits ARID)!"

Arrogate (verb): to unrightfully take or claim. 3

Think: A ROGUE ATE.

My liege – A ROGUE ATE my rations – may I have more since he ARROGATED what was rightfully mine?

Articulate (adjective): using clear, expressive language. 1

Think: ARTICLE.

Oscar Wilde was so ARTICULATE that his conversational speech could be used as a newspaper ARTICLE without any editing.

Artifice (noun): deception; trickery. 2

Think: ARTIFICIAL.

In *The Hunger Games*, Effie Trinket tries to win people over with ARTIFICE, but it doesn't work because her sweetness is so ARTIFICIAL.

Artless (adjective): simple; without cunning. 2

Think: ART-LESS flirting.

Flirting is an ART I use LESS than most people; it's definitely pretty ARTLESS when I just go up to a girl and tell her I like her.

Ascendancy (noun): dominance; superiority. 2

Think: ASCEND.

If you ASCEND the corporate ladder and become chairman of the board, you'll enjoy ASCENDANCY.

Ascetic (adjective): practicing self-denial. 2

Think: ASSET? ICK!

The ASECTIC Buddhist monk, when offered the chance to take money or another ASSET, said "ICK!"

Ashen (adjective): very pale. 1

Think: ASH.

When he saw the ghost, his complexion became so ASHEN that his face was the color of ASH.

Askew (adjective): slanted to one side. 1

Think: SKEW.

Your picture is ASKEW because the earthquake SKEWED it from hanging evenly.

Asperity (noun): bad temper. 3

Think: A SPEAR IN ME.

I have ASPERITY because I have A SPEAR IN ME – can you blame me?

Aspersion (noun): a false claim intended to harm. 2

Think: ASP POISON.

Her ASPERSIONS about what I did last night felt like ASP POISON.

Assail (verb): to attack violently. 2

Think: ASS SAIL.

Come at me, bro: if I ASSAIL you, I'll make your ASS SAIL out the window.

Assiduous (adjective): hardworking; dedicated. 2

Think: ASSIST US.

ASSIDUOUS Sid worked his ass off to ASSIST US.

Assuage: (verb): to make less severe. 2

Think: MASSAGE.

Getting a long MASSAGE will ASSUAGE those sore muscles.

Astute (adjective): clever. 2

Think: SAT STUDENT.

I had a SAT STUDENT named Stu who was so ASTUTE that he got a 2400 on the SAT.

Audacious (adjective): fearlessly bold; arrogantly bold. 1

Audacity

Think: AWED US.

Walking up to Obama and swiping his pen as he was about to sign the bill was so AUDACIOUS that it AWED US.

August (adjective): majestic. 2

Think: AUGUSTUS Caesar.

AUGUSTUS Caesar, the first Roman emperor, was so AUGUST that they named a month after him.

Auspicious (adjective): favorable. 2

Think: SUSPICIOUS I'm AWESOME.

Dude, the chances she'll go out with me are AUSPICIOUS or "ΛWE-spicious" because I'm suspicious that I'm AWESOME.

Austere (adjective): plain; strict; serious; cold. 1

Think: AUSTRIA STERN.

Life among the Alps in AUSTRIA is STERN and AUSTERE - it's hard to party when there's a wind chill of -20.

Automaton (noun): one who acts in a robotic way. 2

Think: AUTOMATION.

Working on assembly line where AUTOMATION has replaced creativity can make you feel like an AUTOMATON.

Avaricious (adjective): greedy. 2

Think: HAVE OUR RICHES.

My boy band and I don't trust you as an agent - you're AVARICIOUS and just want to HAVE OUR RICHES.

Aver (verb): to state confidently; to declare. 2

Think: VERIFY.

After I VERIFY that the blood sample from the crime scene matches your DNA, I'll AVER that you are the killer.

Avuncular (adjective): like an uncle. 2

Think: UNCLE.

The AVUNCULAR professor was like an UNCLE to him, dispensing well-intentioned advice.

Badger (verb): to annoy or pester. 2

Think: BAD JERK.

Good jerks can get laughs, but a BAD JERK will just BADGER you with his attempts at humor.

Banal (adjective): unoriginal. 1

Think: BAN ALL.

The BANAL librarian thought there were enough books already and wanted to BAN ALL the new ones.

Bauble (noun): a small, inexpensive piece of jewelry or toy. 2

Think: BOBBLEHEAD.

The BAUBLE that my favorite baseball player gave me was a BOBBLEHEAD of himself.

Beatific (adjective): extremely happy. 2

Think: BEAUTIFUL! TERRIFIC!

If you feel BEATIFIC, you probably walk around exclaiming, "BEAUTIFUL! TERRIFIC!" all day.

Beatify (verb): to bless; to make happy. 3

Think: BEAUTIFUL home = happiness.

The makeover will BEAUTIFY your home and BEATIFY your family.

Becalm (verb): to make motionless; to soothe. 2

Think: BE CALM!

When my 3-year-old is running around causing havoc, I usually whisper "BE CALM!" to BECALM him.

Bedlam (noun): a state of uproar and confusion. 2

Think: BED LAMB.

It was complete BEDLAM when I entered my hotel room and saw that the BED had a LAMB sleeping in it.

Beguile (verb): to trick. 2

Think: BE GULLIBLE.

BE GULLIBLE, and you'll be easy to BEGUILE.

Behemoth (noun): something huge. 2

Think: BEAST MAMMOTH.

One really large BEAST was the woolly MAMMOTH, a BEHEMOTH that lived during the Ice Age.

Belied (verb): contradicted. 2

Think: LIED.

The used car salesman's smooth manner was BELIED by his sweaty handshake and made me think, "He LIED!"

Belittle (verb): to put down; to disparage. 1

Think: BE LITTLE.

When you say "Good boy!" and pat me on head, you BELITTLE me and make me feel as if I BE LITTLE.

Belligerant
Bellicose (adjective): warlike; inclined to fight. 2

Think: BELLY BELLOW.

"ARRGHH!" When I heard the beast's BELLY BELLOW, I knew it was BELLICOSE.

Bemoan (verb): to mourn over; to express grief for. 2

Think: MOAN.

I BE MOANIN' about the new laws restricting what we can smoke - my friends BEMOAN the legislation, too.

Beneficence (noun): the quality of being kind or charitable. 2

Think: BENEFIT SENT.

Through the BENEFICENCE of musicians like Paul McCartney and Sting, the BENEFIT concert SENT millions of dollars to starving children.

Bereft (adjective): deprived or robbed of something. 2

Think: HE LEFT.

After HE LEFT her at the altar and crushed her dreams, she felt completely BEREFT.

Bifurcated (verb): split in two. 2

Think: BY FORKING.

BY FORKING, the road BIFURCATED into the popular road and the road less traveled by.

Bilious (adjective): bad-tempered. 2

Think: BULLY US.

We goth kids are only BILIOUS because the jocks like to BULLY US.

Blase (adjective): apathetic; unconcerned. 1

Think: BLAH SAY.

I'm a rock star, so I'm BLASE and "BLAH BLAH BLAH" is all I SAY even when blazingly hot girls try to talk to me.

Bloviated (verb): was wordy/windy when speaking. 3

Think: BLOW hot air.

In Harry Potter, Gilderoy Lockhart BLOVIATED; he would BLOW a lot of hot air without much meaning.

Bludgeon (verb): to hit forcefully. 2

Think: BLUDGERS.

In Quidditch, the BLUDGERS are 10-inch, black, iron balls that fly around and sometimes BLUDGEON players.

Bonhomie (noun): a pleasant and friendly mood. 3

Think: ABUNDANCE of HOMIES.

When I have an ABUNDANCE of HOMIES, I have BONHOMIE.

Boor (noun): a crude person with rude, clumsy manners. 1

Think: BOAR manners.

The BOOR had table manners like a wild BOAR and ate directly off the plate with his mouth.

Bootless (adjective): useless. 3

Think: BOOTY-LESS.

A BOOTY-LESS pirate is probably a BOOTLESS pirate.

Bowdlerize (verb): to cut out all the offensive parts of a book. 3

Think: BOULDER-IZE.

Originally, they would BOWDLERIZE Huckleberry Finn so much that they might as well have let BOULDERS roll over the book and tear out half the pages.

Bravado (noun): a false show of bravery; swagger. 1

Think: BRAVE AVOCADO.

Though its trash-talking seemed BRAVE, the AVOCADO and its BRAVADO didn't scare me, since I knew it was just a piece of fruit.

Brazen (adjective): shamelessly bold. 1

Think: BLAZIN'.

BLAZIN' up a joint during class is certainly BRAZEN, but it'll get you expelled 100 out of 100 times.

Brevity (noun): shortness of duration. 1

Think: ABBREVIATE.

I know your speech is brief but ABBREVIATE it even more - this professor actually awards points for BREVITY.

Brusque (adjective): abrupt; curt; harsh. 2

Think: BRUSHED OFF.

I tried to make friends with the club's bouncer, but he was BRUSQUE and BRUSHED me off.

Bucolic (adjective): rustic; rural. 3

Think: BLUE COLLAR.

I'm just a BUCOLIC broccoli farmer - a BLUE COLLAR worker - I don't understand what those suits are talking about!

Bugbear (noun): something to fear. 4

Think: BUG a BEAR.

If you BUG a BEAR, you'll soon have a very serious
BUGBEAR.

Bumptious (adjective): assertive in a loud, arrogant way. 2

Aaron

Think: BUMP US.

You're the type of guy who would push past us in a crowd
and BUMP US and not say you're sorry – you're
BUMPTIOUS.

Burgeoning (adjective): growing. 2

Think: BURGERS.

If you eat too many BURGERS, your waistline will be
BURGEONING.

Buttress (noun): a support. 2

Think: BUTT REST.

The stone column is both a BUTTRESS and a BUTT REST
for tired people to lean against.

Bygone (adjective): past. 2

Think: BYE GONE.

The BYGONE days of my childhood are days I've said BYE to cause they're GONE.

Byzantine (adjective): devious; complicated. 3

Think: BUSY ANT.

Only the BUSY ANT will be able to make its way through the BYZANTINE maze you've created.

Cache (noun): a secure storage place or something in that place. 1

Think: CASH hiding place.

The drug dealer kept his CASH in a CACHE under the bed - he didn't trust banks.

Cacophony (noun): a harsh, unharmonious sound. 2

Think: COUGH SYMPHONY.

The sounds from the tuberculosis ward were a
CACOPHONY - an unpleasant COUGH SYMPHONY.

Cadge (verb): to beg or get via begging. 3

The Prisoner cadged for food

Think: locked in a CAGE.

From her cage.

If you're locked in a CAGE, you'll CADGE for food and
water.

Cajole (verb): to coax. 2

Think: CAGE HOLE.

At the vet, I have to CAJOLE my cat out of the CAGE
HOLE so he can get examined.

Calamitous (adjective): related to a terrible event. 2

Think: CALAMARI VOMIT.

It's CALAMITOUS when you eat undercooked CALAMARI, become VOMITOUS, and puke on your date.

Callous (adjective): unsympathetic; hard-hearted. 2

Think: CALLUS.

The CALLOUS dictator thought nothing of executing his rivals; he must have had a CALLUS on his soul.

Callow (adjective): inexperienced; immature. 2

Think: SHALLOW.

Popping her gum while reading Cosmo, the CALLOW teenager was SHALLOW only because she hadn't seen much of the world yet.

Camaraderie (noun): togetherness. 2

Think: COMRADES.

The Russian camera factory workers shared a sense of CAMARADERIE, calling each other COMRADES.

Capacious (adjective): spacious. 2

Think: Batman's CAPE is SPACIOUS.

Batman is a big guy, so his CAPE is SPACIOUS and CAPACIOUS.

Capitulate (verb): to surrender. 2

Think: CAPSIZED? IT'S TOO LATE.

Once your boat has CAPSIZED, IT'S TOO LATE to think about winning the race: CAPITULATE and just try not to drown.

Capricious (adjective): impulsive; done without forethought. 2

Think: CAPRI PANTS.

Jenny made the CAPRICIOUS decision to buy five pairs of CAPRI PANTS, which she later regretted when they went out of style.

Captious (adjective): overly critical. 3

Think: red CAPS.

Our English teacher is CAPTIOUS: our papers come back with lots of red writing that's in ALL CAPS.

Cardinal (adjective): of main importance. 2

Think: CARDINAL bird.

You'd think the bright red male CARDINAL (noun) was the most CARDINAL (adjective) bird because of its vivid color.

Castigate (verb): to criticize severely. 2

Think: CASTRATE.

The worst way for a Mafia boss to CASTIGATE someone is to CASTRATE him.

Caterwaul (verb): to cry or to complain loudly. 2

Think: CAT WAIL.

If it's in heat, a CAT will WAIL loudly and sometimes CATERWAUL all night long.

Celerity (noun): quickness. 2

Think: ACCELERATE.

After Cee Lo switched to an all-celery diet, he lost 30 pounds and his ability to ACCELERATE increased, as did his CELERITY.

Censure (verb): to criticize harshly. 2

Think: CENSOR.

If you really wanted to CENSURE your rival's editorial you could just CENSOR it completely.

Cerebral (adjective): intellectual. 2

Think: CEREBRUM.

Einstein was so CEREBRAL that they studied the CEREBRUM of his brain after he died.

Chagrin (noun): distress caused by disappointment. 2

Think: CHUGGIN' TRAGIC.

You won't believe this, but to my CHAGRIN, Chad is CHUGGIN' a bottle of mouthwash right now – this is a TRAGIC date.

Champion (verb): to fight for. 2

Think: CHAMPION (noun).

If you CHAMPION (verb) that turtle in the turtle race and cheer for her really loudly, it's more likely she'll become the CHAMPION (noun).

Chary (adjective): very cautious. 2

Think: CHAIR-WARY.

My brothers were always pulling my CHAIR away as I was about to sit down, so now I'm CHARY, or CHAIR-WARY.

Chicanery (noun): trickery. 3

Think: CHICK-GAIN-ERY

Your frat brother's feigned interest in that cute girl's paintings was clearly CHICANERY; his motive was "CHICK-GAIN-ERY".

Choleric (adjective): irritable. 2

Think: CHOLERA.

I'd be CHOLERIC too if someone's fecal matter made me get CHOLERA.

Churlish (adjective): rude; difficult. 2

Think: CHURCH LUSH.

The CHURCH LUSH usually showed up to mass stumbling drunk, inviting us to call him CHURLISH.

Circuitous (adjective): roundabout; not direct. 2

Think: CIRCUIT-ISH.

The crooked cabdriver took a CIRCUITOUS route; his path was CIRCUIT-ISH to increase the fare.

Circumscribed (adjective): restricted. 2

Think: CIRCUMFERENCE SCRIBE.

The evil SCRIBE drew a magical CIRCUMFERENCE around our campsite, which CIRCUMSCRIBED our movement to that circle.

Circumspect (adjective): cautious. 2

Think: CIRCLE INSPECT.

When you rent a car, walk in a CIRCLE to INSPECT it for dents; if you're not CIRCUMSPECT now, they may charge you later.

Circumvents (verb): avoids; gets around something. 2

Think: CIRCUMFERENCE VENTS.

She CIRCUMVENTS the guards by crawling around the enemy base's CIRCUMFERENCE through the VENTS.

Clandestine (adjective): secret. 2

Think: CLAN of DESTINY.

Because we're the CLAN of DESTINY, we have to keep our meetings CLANDESTINE – otherwise, the empire will kill us all.

Clemency (noun): mercy. 2

Think: CLEMENS MERCY.

The pitcher Roger CLEMENS was shown MERCY by the jury and found not guilty - an act of CLEMENCY, since he was accused of taking steroids.

Cloying (adjective): gross because it's too much. 2

Think: ANNOYING.

Always talking baby-talk to each other, the couple was so ANNOYING that they were CLOYING.

Cocksure (adjective): overconfident. 2

Think: COCKY and SURE.

The baseball rookie was so COCKY and SURE that he'd hit a home run during his first at-bat that he was COCKSURE.

Coddle (adjective): to treat with excessive care. 2

Think: CUDDLE.

The mother dog would CODDLE and CUDDLE her puppy so much that I thought it would never learn to fend for itself.

Coerced (verb): forced. 2

Think: COOPERATE by FORCE.

I didn't want to leave the bar, but the bouncer COERCED me to COOPERATE by using FORCE.

Cognizant (adjective): aware; informed. 2

Think: RECOGNIZE.

If you're COGNIZANT of our theory, you must RECOGNIZE where our solution came from.

Cohesive (adjective): holding together well. 1

Think: ADHESIVE.

A COHESIVE argument holds together even when attacked – as if it's strengthened by an ADHESIVE.

Coin (verb): to invent a new word or phrase. 2

Think: COIN (noun).

Just as the U.S. mint molds metal into a new COIN (noun), so we can COIN (verb) new expressions.

Commensurate (adjective): equal or proportionate. 2

Think: CO-MEASURE IT.

Our estimates of the carbon content of this dinosaur bone will be COMMENSURATE if we CO-MEASURE IT.

Commiserate (verb): to sympathize with. 2

Think: MISERY loves COMPANY.

Come COMMISERATE with us - MISERY loves COMPANY.

Companionable (adjective): sociable; friendly. 2

Think: COMPANION-ABLE.

Most dogs are COMPANIONABLE and love people; that's why they're so ABLE to be COMPANIONS.

Complicit (adjective): involved in a crime. 2

Think: ACCOMPLICE.

Though I robbed the bank and my ACCOMPLICE just drove me there, he was considered COMPLICIT by the law.

Composure (noun): calmness. 1

Think: COMPOSER'S CALM POSE.

Even though he was performing his music for kings and queens, the composer's CALM POSE showed his COMPOSURE.

Compunction (noun): regret, remorse. 3

Think: PUNCTURED balloon.

I felt COMPUNCTION after accidentally PUNCTURING the child's birthday balloon and making him cry.

Concomitant (adjective): accompanying, especially in a less important way. 3

Think: CAN COME WITH IT.

Drinking too much carries the CONCOMITANT risk of depression that CAN COME WITH IT.

Concord (noun): harmony. 2

Think: CONCURRED.

We all CONCURRED that we should go into the grape jelly business, so it's no surprise that our company is enjoying a feeling of CONCORD.

Concupiscence (noun): strong desire, esp. sexual desire. 3

Think: CUPID'S ESSENCE.

If you have CONCUPISCENCE, you have CUPID'S ESSENCE running through your veins.

Condign (adjective): deserved; appropriate. 3

Think: CAN DIG.

I CAN DIG the murderer's conviction because it was CONDIGN.

Condones (verb): allows something that is bad. 1

Think: CON DONE.

The CON DONE it because the lazy warden CONDONES misbehavin'.

Conflagration (noun): a fire. 2

Think: burning FLAG NATION.

There is a debate about the FLAG in our NATION - is it legal to use the Stars and Stripes for a CONFLAGRATION?

Conflate (verb): to confuse. 2

Think: CON INFLATED.

The CON artist INFLATED the value of the racehorse by grooming it, making me CONFLATE sleek appearance with speed.

Conniving (verb): secretly plotting to do bad things. 2

Think: Mean girls' KNIVES.

Mean girls act nice, but don't be CONNED: they're CONNIVING to stick KNIVES in your back.

Connoisseur (noun): an expert; one who knows the subtleties of a subject. 1

Think: CAN KNOW SIR.

When it comes to breakdancing, call me "CAN KNOW SIR" because I'm a CONNOISSEUR of the art.

Conscientious (adjective): driven by the urge to do what's right; careful. 2

Think: CONSCIENCES.

CONSCIENTIOUS people usually are driven to do good deeds by their CONSCIENCES.

Consternation (noun): confusion; agitation; dismay. 2

Think: CONCERNED NATION.

On 9/11/01, a CONCERNED NATION stood in CONSTERNATION watching the aftermath of terrorism.

Contumacious (adjective): stubbornly disobedient; rebellious. 3

Think: CONTRARY TUMMY.

I have a CONTRARY TUMMY – it's CONTUMACIOUS and gives me indigestion if I try to eat spicy food.

Conundrum (noun): a difficult problem. 2

Think: NUN DRUM.

Building a NUN DRUM is a CONUNDRUM because nuns don't like loud noises.

Conversant (adjective): familiar with. 2

Think: CONVERSE IT.

If you're CONVERSANT with something, you can CONVERSE about it intelligently.

Copious (adjective): plentiful. 1

Think: COPY US.

If the zombie apocalypse happens and we survive, let's hope cloning can COPY US and make humans more COPIOUS.

Cordial (adjective): affectionate. 1

Think: CORDIAL (noun).

The alcohol in the CORDIAL (noun) made me act more CORDIAL (adjective).

Cordon (verb): to enclose, either to restrict or to protect. 2

Think: CORD ON.

CORDON off that area by tying a CORD ON and around all the trees so people know it's off limits.

Corroborate (verb): to support with evidence. 2

Think: CO-ROBBER.

When robbing a bank, use a CO-ROBBER who will CORROBORATE your story.

Cosmopolitan (adjective): sophisticated. 2

Think: COSMO.

After reading the dating advice in COSMO, the 14-year-old thought she was quite COSMOPOLITAN.

Covert (adjective): not openly shown. 2

Think: COVERED.

The CIA agent was on a COVERT mission, so he COVERED his true identity.

Cowed (adjective): intimidated. 2

Think: COWARD.

The bully was at heart a COWARD: as soon as I stood up to him he was COWED into silence.

Crepuscular (adjective): related to twilight. 3

Think: CREEPY MUSCULAR.

In the movie Twilight, CREEPY, MUSCULAR vampires prowl during the CREPUSCULAR hours of the evening.

Crestfallen (adjective): dejected; depressed. 2

Think: CREST FALLEN.

When I saw that my CREST toothpaste had FALLEN off my brush into the sink, I was CRESTFALLEN since that was a waste of perfectly good toothpaste.

Cryptic (adjective): having an unclear or hidden meaning. 1

Think: CRYPT.

Scrawled in blood on the wall of the mummy's CRYPT, the CRYPTIC hieroglyphics both confused and frightened us.

Culpable (adjective): deserving blame. 2

Think: CULPRIT.

Unsurprisingly, the cop thought the CULPRIT was
CULPABLE.

Cumbersome (adjective): awkward due to large size. 1

Think: CUCUMBER.

It felt CUMBERSOME to walk down the beach with a
gigantic CUCUMBER down the front of my Speedo.

Cupidity (noun): greedy desire for. 3

Think: CUPID.

After being shot by CUPID'S arrow, Sarah developed such
CUPIDITY for her valentine that she called him daily.

Curmudgeon (noun): a grumpy old man. 2

Think: CURSE MUD.

Only a CURMUDGEON would CURSE the MUD in the
garden on this sunny spring day.

Curtail (verb): to lessen. 2

Think: CUT off your TAIL.

If you really want to win this lizard beauty pageant, you've got to be shorter. CURTAIL your length - CUT off your TAIL.

Cynosure (noun): something that guides or stands out. 4

Think: SIGN to be SURE.

Polaris (the North Star) was a CYNOSURE for ancient sailors, a SIGN they could be SURE of.

Daunt (verb): to intimidate or discourage. 1

Think: DON'T!

My mean old aunt Mildred would often DAUNT me when I was younger by screaming, "DON'T!" whenever I got too loud.

Dearth (noun): lack. 2

Think: DEAD EARTH.

Due to the DEAD EARTH of our farmland, there will be a DEARTH of food this winter.

Debauchery (noun): extreme indulgence in pleasure. 2

Think: THE BACHELOR PARTY.

During THE BACHELOR PARTY, the wolf pack in The Hangover participated in some serious DEBAUCHERY.

Debilitate (verb): to weaken. 2

Think: DECREASE ABILITY.

Cancer will often DEBILITATE its victims and can DECREASE their ABILITY to be active.

Decadent (adjective): decaying; self-indulgent. 1

Think: DECAYED.

In *WALL-E*, the DECADENT passengers of the spaceship have DECAYED into overweight, lazy, passive lumps.

Decimate (verb): to destroy a large part of. 2

Think: DECIMAL REMAINS.

At the start of our campaign, all of our soldiers were healthy, but attacks and disease have DECIMATED the ranks so that only a DECIMAL REMAINS alive.

Declaimed (verb): spoke loudly and self-importantly. 2

Think: "I DECLARE!"

"Well, I DECLARE!" the southern belle DECLAIMED.

Decorous (adjective): well-behaved. 2

Think: THE CHORUS.

Kids in THE CHORUS are usually not rebels - they're often DECOROUS.

Decrepit (adjective): worn-out; run-down. 2

Think: SCRAP IT.

Your DECREPIT old car looks like crap; you should SCRAP IT.

Decried (verb): expressed strong disapproval about. 2

Think: CRIED.

After my boss DECRIED my work in front of everyone, I went home and CRIED.

Defamatory (adjective): something that hurts someone's reputation. 2

Think: DE-FAME.

The DEFAMATORY Enquirer story will "DE-FAME" that actor; he'll lose his fame.

Defenestrate (verb): to quickly throw out. 3

Think: DEFENSE DEMONSTRATE.

If you DEFENESTRATE a burglar through a plate-glass window, your home DEFENSE is DEMONSTRATED.

Defunct (adjective): no longer existing. 2

Think: DE-FUNCTION.

When I can fly in my dreams, the law of gravity seems to be DEFUNCT, like it has been "DE-FUNCTIONED".

Delectable (adjective): delightful; delicious. 1

Think: DELICIOUS ELECTABLE.

Ryan Gosling should run for president since most women think he's DELECTABLE and DELICIOUS enough to be ELECTABLE.

Deleterious (adjective): harmful. 2

Think: DELETES.

Using that old computer could be DELETERIOUS to your grade since it randomly DELETES files.

Demagogue (noun): a leader who gains power by trickery. 2

Think: DEMIGOD.

The cult was led by a DEMAGOGUE; he manipulated followers into thinking he was a DEMIGOD.

Demarcate (verb): to define; to set apart. 2

Think: MARK IT.

If you want to DEMARCATE your side of the dorm room, MARK IT with a long piece of masking tape.

Demotic (adjective): popular; common. 3

Think: DEMOCRATIC.

Obama uses DEMOTIC language in his speeches to seem more DEMOCRATIC.

Demur (verb): to object. 2

Think: MURMUR.

Though no one has spoken up yet, THE MURMUR from the class suggests they DEMUR to my idea that they do more homework.

Denigrate (verb): to attack the reputation of or to put down. 2

Think: DENY I'M GREAT.

If you DENY I'm GREAT, you DENIGRATE me.

Denizen (noun): inhabitant; one who is often at a place. 2

Think: DEN CITIZEN.

One of the DENIZENS of the caves in my woods is a black bear - he's a bear DEN CITIZEN.

Denuded (verb): stripped bare. 3

Think: NUDE.

Loggers DENUDED the forested rise, felling trees and trampling undergrowth until it was just an NUDE hill of earth.

Deplete (verb): to use up. 1

Think: DELETE.

DEPLETED uranium has had some of its radioactivity DELETED.

Depredate (verb): to take by force; to ravage; to ruin. 3

Think: PREDATOR.

The PREDATORS in the forest will DEPREDATE your village's livestock if you don't build a really good fence and get guard dogs.

Deride (verb): to make fun of. 2

Think: DEE'S RIDE.

We all DERIDE DEE'S RIDE - it's a brown 1987 Buick with ghetto rims.

Descry (verb): to catch sight of; to discover. 2

Think: DESCRIBE.

Ok, now that I DESCRY the iceberg that we're sailing towards, I can DESCRIBE it to you.

Desecrate (verb): to violate something sacred. 2

Think: DE-SACRED.

If you peed on an altar, you would DESECRATE it, or "DE-SACRED" it - it would no longer be sacred.

Desiccated (adjective): dried out. 2

Think: DESERT SICK.

The DESERT made me SICK because the dry heat DESICCATED my body.

Despoiled (verb): stripped of value. 2

Think: SPOILED.

Desperate for oil, the U.S. drilled in Alaska and DESPOILED the land, and act which SPOILED it for future generations.

Despot (noun): an all-powerful ruler. 2

Think: DESPICABLE.

History has shown us that DESPOTS - like Kim Jong Il - are often DESPICABLE human beings.

Desuetude (noun): disuse. 4

Think: DISUSE ATTITUDE.

The unnecessary security guard at the knitting store had an air of lazy DESUETUDE about him - kind of a DISUSE ATTITUDE.

Devoid (adjective): completely lacking. 1

Think: THE VOID.

THE VOID of deep space is DEVOID of air, warmth, or life.

Dexterity (adjective): skill; good coordination. 1

Think: DEXTER.

The fictional serial killer DEXTER has a grisly
DEXTERITY about the way he kills people.

Diabolical (adjective): devilish. 1

Think: DIE ABOLISH.

Your law that makes cigarettes part of school lunches is
DIABOLICAL and will cause children to DIE... ABOLISH
it!

Diaphanous (adjective): so flimsy as to be see-through. 3

Think: DIANA'S FAN.

Princess DIANA's delicate rice-paper FAN was
DIAPHANOUS.

Diatribe (noun): an angry speech. 2

Think: DIE TRIBE.

I didn't understand the words of his DIATRIBE, but I guessed the native said I'd DIE from his TRIBE killing me.

Didactic (adjective): designed to teach. 2

Think: DICTIONARY TACTIC.

The definitions in a DICTIONARY use the TACTIC of explaining words clearly in order to be DIDACTIC.

Diffident (adjective): timid. 2

Think: DIFFICULT DENTURES.

I'm DIFFIDENT when in public because I'm self-conscious about how weird my DIFFICULT DENTURES look.

Dilatory (adjective): tending to procrastinate. 2

Think: DELAY LATER.

The DILATORY gator liked to DELAY things until LATER.

Dilettante (noun): a dabbler; one with superficial knowledge of an area. 2

Think: DILUTED.

The DILETTANTE's knowledge of the subject was, understandably, DILUTED.

Dint (noun): force; power. 2

Think: Hulk's DENT.

The Incredible Hulk made a DENT in the car by DINT of his enormous strength.

Discomfit (verb): to embarrass or confuse. 2

Think: DISCOMFORT.

Realizing one's suit had been replaced with a too-tight Speedo would DISCOMFORT and DISCOMFIT anyone.

Disconcert (verb): to confuse or frustrate. 2

Think: DISS the CONCERT.

To liven up recitals, I DISCONCERT the musicians by DISSING the CONCERT.

Discreet (adjective): having or showing self-restraint and good judgment. 1

Think: THIS SECR**ET**.

I'm pregnant - but please, be DISCRE**ET** and keep THIS SECR**ET** - if my parents find out, they'll kill me.

Discrete (adjective): individually distinct; separate. 1

Think: CRETE.

The Greek island of CRETE is DIS**CRETE** because it doesn't touch any other land.

Discriminate (verb): to notice subtle variations. 2

Think: one meaning is criminal; one is neutral.

DISCRIMINATE (verb), so you'll know when "discriminate" is about prejudice and when it's about noticing.

Disgruntled (adjective): displeased. 2

Think: GRUNTED.

The fat warthog GRUNTED to show he was DIS**GRUNTLED** with his small dinner.

Dismissive (adjective): showing rejection and contempt for. 1

Think: DISMISS.

When she sings "Call Me Maybe", Carly Rae Jepsen is DISMISSIVE because she DISMISSED all the other boys who tried to chase her.

Disparage (verb): to insult or put down. 2

Think: DESPAIR and RAGE.

He felt DESPAIR and RAGE because the rapper liked to diss and DISPARAGE him.

Dispatch (noun): speed; efficiency. 2

Think: DISPATCHER.

If you want a job as a DISPATCHER - using the radio to direct police - you'd better have DISPATCH.

Disputatious (adjective): inclined to argue. 2

Think: DISPUTE.

After being pulled over, the DISPUTATIOUS lawyer unwisely DISPUTED the accuracy of the cop's radar gun.

Dissemble (verb): to mislead, hide or conceal. 2

Think: DISASSEMBLE gun.

The terrorist tried to DISSEMBLE his plan by DISASSEMBLING his gun before trying to smuggle it through airport security.

Disseminated (verb): spread out. 2

Think: DISS 'EM, NATE.

His dad advised to "DISS 'EM, NATE", so Nate DISSEMINATED flyers all over the school that criticized his opponents in the election.

Distension (noun): swelling. 2

Think: DIS-TENSION.

A belly showing DISTENSION after a huge meal might be because the person has weak abs with no muscle TENSION.

Dither (verb): to stress out from indecision. 2

Think: DITZ DO EITHER.

You're such a DITZ – you'd DO EITHER and it's making you DITHER.

Diurnal (adjective): daily; of the daytime. 3

Think: The URINAL.

My use of the URINAL is DIURNAL – I pee every day.

Divisive (adjective): creating disunity. 2

Think: DIVIDE.

Yoko Ono had a DIVISIVE effect on The Beatles, DIVIDING the group into two parts.

Docile (adjective): Calm, even-tempered. 2

Think: DOCTOR.

The DOCILE DOCTOR remained calm even though his patient was clinging to life by a thread.

Doggedness (noun): stubborn determination. 2

Think: DOG-NESS.

The fighter's DOGGEDNESS, even after he was knocked down, was like that of a fearless BULLDOG.

Doggerel (noun): poorly written verse. 2

Think: DOG VERSE.

Most Valentine's Day card poems are such DOGGEREL that it seems as though DOGS wrote the VERSE.

Dogmatic (adjective): stubborn; inflexible. 2

Think: DOG bath.

My DOG AUTOMATICALLY becomes DOGMATIC if you try to give him a bath, since he hates water.

Dolorous (adjective): sad; mournful. 2

Think: DOLORES'S DOLDRUMS.

I'd be DOLOROUS and in the DOLDRUMS too if my name were DOLORES.

Dormant (adjective): temporarily inactive. 1

Think: DOORMAN.

If you work as a DOORMAN, you know that most of the time you're just standing there, DORMANT.

Dour (adjective): gloomy; stern. 2

Think: SOUR.

The teacher's DOUR expression made her pupils feel SOUR.

Draconian (adjective): cruelly strict. 3

Think: DRACO Malfoy.

If DRACO Malfoy had taught the Gryffindor students, I'm sure he would have been a DRACONIAN instructor.

Droll (adjective): funny. 2

Think: ROLL (with laughter).

DROLL humor makes me ROLL with laughter.

Dubious (adjective): doubtful or suspect. 1

Think: DUBSTEP.

I am DUBIOUS as to whether the DUBSTEP music trend is going to last.

Dudgeon (noun): a tantrum caused by being offended. 4

Think: DUNGEON GRUDGE.

I was in high DUDGEON after they threw me in the DUNGEON for jaywalking, and I held a GRUDGE.

Dupe (verb): to trick. 2

Think: DOPE.

A DOPE is easy to DUPE.

Duplicitous (adjective): deceptive. 3

Think: DUPLICATE-NESS.

Politicians try to make everyone like them, but their two-faced DUPLICATE-NESS is DUPLICITOUS.

Dyspeptic (adjective): grumpy. 3

Think: PEPTO-Bismol.

This PEPTO-Bismol will prevent indigestion and the resulting DYSPEPTIC mood.

Ebullient (adjective): excitedly enthusiastic. 2

Think: RED BULL.

After I chugged a giant RED BULL, I felt extremely EBULLIENT.

Eclectic (adjective): varied. 2

Think: SELECTION COLLECTION.

If your musical tastes are ECLECTIC, I can probably name any style SELECTION and you'll say it's in your COLLECTION.

Effaced (verb): made less visible. 2

Think: ERASED.

On old nickels, Thomas Jefferson's face is often EFFACED to the point of almost being ERASED.

Effete (adjective): without strength or vitality; weak; soft. 3

Think: FEEBLE.

The former athlete became EFFETE and FEEBLE from years of just sitting on the couch.

.

Efficacious (adjective): effective. 2

Think: EFFECTIVENESS.

If you have senioritis, a brief vacation is an EFFICACIOUS way to increase your EFFECTIVENESS.

Effluvium (noun): an invisible, often harmful, vapor. 3

Think: FLU.

The EFFLUVIUM coming from the FLU patient's mouth infected the nurse.

Effrontery (noun): shameless boldness. 2

Think: FRONTING HOMIES.

What's with these homies dissin' my girl? Why do they gotta FRONT? (Because they have EFFRONTERY, Weezer.)

Effusive (adjective): extremely expressive. 2

Think: FUSSY.

Imagine if Nicki Minaj was your grandma? She's so EFFUSIVE she'd make a FUSS over your every accomplishment.

Egalitarian (adjective): based on the belief in human equality. 2

Think: EQUAL EAGLE.

In the U.S., our EGALITARIAN belief that all men are created EQUAL is symbolized by the bald EAGLE.

Egregious (adjective): bad in an obvious way. 2

Think: OUTRAGEOUS.

Her saying that she had to wash her hamster was such an EGREGIOUS and OUTRAGEOUS excuse that it made me say "Jesus!"

Eldritch (adjective): weird; eerie. 3

Think: ELF-WITCH.

The ELF-WITCH Galadriel in <u>The Lord Of The Rings</u> was ELDRITCH because of her ability to speak inside our heads.

Embellish (verb): to decorate. 1

Think: BELLS.

Hanging little BELLS all over your home is one (weird) way to EMBELLISH it.

Embroiled (verb): in a difficult situation. 2

Think: ON BROIL.

I was EMBROILED in a dangerous situation when I got locked in an oven set on "BROIL".

Embryonic (adjective): in an early stage. 2

Think: EMBRYO.

It's pretty obvious that a human EMBRYO is EMBRYONIC when compared to an adult human.

Emollient (adjective): soothing. 2

Think: EMO.

Listening to EMO music has an EMOLLIENT effect on my emotions because it's so sensitive.

Emphatic (adjective): forceful. 2

Think: EMPHASIZE.

When I yell at people, I EMPHASIZE every word to be more EMPHATIC about my demands.

Encomium (noun): praise. 3

Think: IN COMIC-CON.

IN COMIC-CON, the entertainment convention, nerds give ENCOMIUM to the latest comic-book movies.

Encompass (verb): to include. 1

Think: COMPASS.

Use this COMPASS to draw a circle around the things you want to ENCOMPASS.

Encroaching (verb): gradually invading one's rights or property. 2

Think: ROACHES.

My apartment's ROACHES are ENCROACHING upon my space: they now occupy the kitchen.

Enervating (adjective): tiring. 2

Think: RENOVATING.

RENOVATING their kitchen by themselves not only got on the couple's nerves, but also was extremely ENERVATING.

Enmity (noun): hatred. 2

Think: ENEMY.

I have ENMITY for my ENEMY - what else would you expect?

Ennui (noun): dissatisfaction resulting from boredom. 2

Think: ENNUI THERE YET?

Take a seven-year-old on a long car ride, and you'll hear the ENNUI in his voice when he repeatedly asks, "ENNUI THERE YET?"

Ensorcelled (adjective): bewitched; enchanted. 4

Think: SORCERER.

The SORCERER ENSORCELLED the adventurers with a powerful spell that made them forget who they were.

Entreat (verb): to plead. 2

Think: IN RETREAT.

IN RETREAT, the fleeing general ENTREATED us to spare his soldiers' lives.

Ephemeral (adjective): fleeting; short-lived. 1

Think: FM FOR ALL.

Since satellite radio is ten times better than normal radio, the days of FM FOR ALL are EPHEMERAL.

Equivocal (adjective): intentionally unclear. 2

Think: EQUALLY VOCAL.

The EQUIVOCAL politician was EQUALLY VOCAL about both sides of the issue.

Eradicate (verb): to wipe out. 2

Think: RADIATE.

You can RADIATE food to ERADICATE the bacteria in it.

Eschew (verb): to avoid. 2

Think: AH-CHOO.

ESCHEW people who say "AH-CHOO!" unless you want to catch their colds.

Esoteric (adjective): known by only a few people. 2

Think: ISOLATED TERRIFIC.

Einstein's ESOTERIC knowledge ISOLATED him from most of his peers since his acumen was so TERRIFIC.

Espouse (verb): to support or to give loyalty to. 2

Think: SPOUSE.

Chances are that you will ESPOUSE your SPOUSE - you married her, so you probably have her back.

Espy (verb): to glimpse; to catch sight of. 3

Think: I SPY.

I SPY something blue - do you ESPY it, too?

Estimable (adjective): worthy. 2

Think: ESTEEM-able.

If someone is ESTIMABLE they are "ESTEEM-ABLE", i.e., they're deserving of your positive regard.

Estranged (verb): separated in a negative way. 2

Think: STRANGER.

Gotye's ESTRANGED girlfriend cut him out and treated him like a STRANGER and it felt so rough.

Ethereal (adjective): delicate; heavenly; insubstantial. 2

Think: OTHER than REAL.

My God, Joyce - your meringue cookies are ETHEREAL - so light, so delicious - they must be something OTHER than REAL.

Etiolated (verb): made pale; weakened. 3

Think: TOILET-ED.

Keeping my goldfish in the bleach-containing TOILET tank violated his trust and ETIOLATED him so much that he turned white.

Euphemism (noun): an inoffensive term used in place of an offensive one. 1

Think: USE FEMINISM.

USE FEMINISM if you're a guy and want to create a EUPHEMISM for PMS – otherwise you might get yourself killed.

Eurytopic (adjective): tolerant of many different environments. 4

Think: EUROPE TROPICS.

That plant is EURYTOPIC because it grows both in cold, rainy EUROPE and in the hot, humid TROPICS.

Evanescent (adjective): fleeting; lasting only briefly. 2

Think: VANISH SCENT.

The cologne's fragrance will VANISH soon; its SCENT is EVANESCENT.

Evinced (verb): revealed. 2

Think: EVIDENCE.

Vince EVINCED the villain by providing EVIDENCE.

Exacerbated (verb): made more severe; aggravated. 2

Think: EXASPERATED.

I'm EXASPERATED - not only did you get us lost in the woods, but you also EXACERBATED the situation by dropping our phone in that swamp.

Exacting (adjective): requiring strict attention to detail. 2

Think: EXACT.

Our EXACTING architecture professor demanded that our model be drawn EXACTLY to scale.

Excoriated (verb): strongly condemned. 2

Think: SCOURED.

Simon Cowell's criticism on American Idol
EXCORIATED the contestant – she felt as if she'd been
SCOURED by a rough dish pad.

Exculpated (verb): freed from blame. 2

Think: EX-CULPRIT.

If you commit a crime but have a clever lawyer, you'll be
EXCULPATED and be an "EX-CULPRIT".

Execrable (adjective): detestable; awful. 3

Think: EXCREMENT.

Your unfunny jokes about EXCREMENT are
EXECRABLE – they're shit.

Exodus (noun): the departure of many people. 1

Think: EXIT US.

During the Syrian civil war, there was a mass EXODUS of
refugees who must have been thinking, "EXIT US!"

Exorbitant (adjective): excessive. 2

Think: EXTRA for ORBIT.

The fancy space hotel charged EXORBITANT fees due to the EXTRA costs needed to ORBIT the earth.

Expatriate (noun): one who has moved to a foreign country. 2

Think: EX-PATRIOT.

We said our EXPATRIATE friend was an anti-American EX-PATRIOT since he moved to France.

Expedient (adjective): helpful in a practical way. 2

Think: SPEEDY.

To be SPEEDY, I booked my flight on Expedia.com; it was more EXPEDIENT than calling the airline.

Exponent (noun): a supporter of something. 3

Think: EX-OPPONENT.

Upon Romney's nomination, McCain became his EXPONENT for the greater good of the GOP and therefore was his EX-OPPONENT.

Expunge (verb): to get rid of. 2

Think: EX with SPONGE.

The best way to make a spill an "EX-spill" is to use a SPONGE to EXPUNGE the mess.

Extant (adjective): present or existing (opposite of extinct). 2

Think: EXISTING ANT.

Since he was about to get stepped on, "I EXIST!" exclaimed the ANT to the elephant.

Extenuating (adjective): less serious due to a partial excuse. 3

Think: EXTENSION.

I got an EXTENSION on my paper because there were EXTENUATING circumstances – I got trampled by an elephant.

Extirpate (verb): to get rid of completely. 3

Think: EXTERMINATE.

If you have pests in your house that you want to EXTIRPATE, call someone who will EXTERMINATE them.

Extol (verb): to praise highly. 2

Think: EX-TOLL.

I EXTOL this highway because it used to charge a toll, but now it's an EX-TOLL road.

Fabricate (verb): to make up in order to deceive. 1

Think: FABRIC background.

The movie set background was FABRICATED, woven from FABRIC to resemble a mountain range.

Facetious (adjective): playfully funny. 2

Think: FACE "E".

The FACETIOUS comedian made us smile so much that our FACES looked like we were constantly saying "E". (try it!)

Fallible (adjective): capable of making an error. 2

Think: FAIL-ABLE.

Jenkins! The rookie agent you picked is FALLIBLE – for him, the mission is extremely FAIL-ABLE.

Fanatic (adjective): full of extreme enthusiasm. 2

Think: FAN LUNATIC.

The FANATIC Green Bay Packers FAN - a LUNATIC - painted his face green and wore a cheesehead hat every day of the year.

Farce (noun): a comical, unrealistic, mocking display or show. 2

Think: FARTS.

I know your play is a FARCE because of how many times the characters FART.

Fastidious (adjective): having very picky standards. 2

Think: FAST TO TIDY.

My roommate is FASTIDIOUS about cleaning; she gets mad if I am not FAST to TIDY UP the apartment.

Fatuous (adjective): lazily foolish. 2

Think: FAT ASS.

If you're FATUOUS about nutrition, you might end up with a FAT ASS.

Fawning (verb) kissing up to. 2

Think: FAWN (baby deer).

The little FAWN's only hope to get the bear to spare its life was by using FAWNING behavior.

Feckless (adjective): weak; worthless; irresponsible. 2

Think: F in CLASS.

If you get an F in CLASS, your study habits were probably FECKLESS.

Fecund (adjective): fruitful; inventive. 2

Think: FECES UNDER.

Spreading manure, i.e., FECES, UNDER your crops as fertilizer will make your harvest FECUND.

Ferret (verb): to bring to light; to uncover. 2

Think: FERRET (the animal).

If you keep a FERRET as a pet, it will FERRET out all your lost earrings since they can crawl under anything.

Fervor (noun): passion. 2

Think: FEVER.

The lovers' FERVOR for each other was so great that their skin felt FEVER-hot.

Festoon (verb): to decorate. 2

Think: FESTIVAL.

The harvest moon FESTIVAL is coming! Time to FESTOON the barn for the big dance!

Fetid (adjective): bad-smelling. 2

Think: FEET.

FEET often are FETID.

Filial (adjective): like a son or daughter. 2

Think: AFFILIATED.

It was the son's FILIAL duty to care for his dying mother since he was AFFILIATED with her by blood.

Finagled (verb): obtained, often through trickery or indirect methods. 2

Think: FINAGLE a BAGEL.

Even though I had lost my wallet, I FINAGLED a BAGEL from the bagel lady by claiming I had invented cream cheese.

Finicky (adjective): difficult to please. 1

Think: NIT-PICKY.

The princess was NIT-PICKY – she was so FINICKY that she refused to sleep on the mattress with a pea under it.

Fitful (adjective): irregular; intermittent. 2

Think: FIT-FULL.

Our new baby only sleeps FITFULLY – the night seems FULL of his crying FITS.

Flagrant (adjective): shockingly bad. 1

Think: FRAGRANT VAGRANT.

No matter what your feelings towards homeless people are, you can't deny that man is a FRAGRANT VAGRANT - his B.O. is so bad it's FLAGRANT.

Fleeting (adjective): short-lived. 1

Think: FLEE.

My stay in the village was by necessity FLEETING: a dragon attacked, and I had to FLEE.

Flippant (adjective): lacking respect or seriousness. 2

Think: FLIP OFF.

If you're FLIPPANT, you probably FLIP people off on a regular basis.

Florid (adjective): overly decorated; reddish. 2

Think: FLOWERED.

The 12-year-old girl's room was FLOWERED with hundreds of red-hued decorations - her style was FLORID.

Flotilla (noun): a fleet of ships. 2

Think: FLOATING around GODZILLA.

FLOATING around GODZILLA was a FLOTILLA from the Japanese navy.

Flotsam (noun): floating debris. 2

Think: FLOAT.

After the Titanic sank, Rose was able to survive by climbing onto a piece of FLOATING FLOTSAM from the wreckage.

Flounder (verb): to act clumsily or ineffectively. 2

Think: FLOP UNDER.

Bad dancers FLOUNDER (verb) through clubs like flounders (noun) that FLOP UNDER the seat of the boat once they're caught.

Flouted (verb): treated without respect. 2

Think: FLUNG OUT.

The rebel FLOUTED the rules so badly that he FLUNG them OUT the window.

Flummoxed (adjective): confused. 2

Think: FLUME OX.

At the water park, I was completely FLUMMOXED when, in the FLUME ride, I saw an OX swimming along.

Foible (noun): a minor weakness of character. 2

Think: FOIL-ABLE.

Your plan to take over the world is FOIL-ABLE because you have many FOIBLES.

Foment (verb): to encourage the growth of. 2

Think: FORM IT!

In *Star Wars*, Princess Leia FOMENTED the rebel group by telling the rebels to "FORM IT!"

Forbearance (noun): patience; tolerance. 2

Think: BEAR TOLERANCE.

I'm usually harsh on people who borrow my money, but for BEARS I have more TOLERANCE and practice FORBEARANCE since they scare me.

Foreground (verb): to highlight. 3

Think: FOREGROUND (noun).

That boy is magic! FOREGROUND (verb) his talent by making sure he's in the FOREGROUND (noun) of the stage!

Forestall (verb): to delay, hinder, or prevent. 1

Think: FOR STALL.

The booby traps I surrounded my fort with will FORESTALL invaders – they're FOR STALLING.

Fortitude (noun): strength. 2

Think: FORTRESS.

The Bulgarian weightlifter's mental FORTITUDE during training gave him a body that looked like a FORTRESS.

Fortuitous (adjective): lucky. 2

Think: FORTUNATE for US.

It was FORTUITOUS and FORTUNATE for us that the polar bear we encountered had just eaten a seal and was too full to eat us.

Fracas (noun): a noisy brawl. 2

Think: FRAT RUCKUS.

The FRAT brothers often caused a RUCKUS by getting into a drunken FRACAS.

Fractious (adjective): cranky. 3

Think: FRACTURE US.

The FRACTIOUS football player is best avoided: if his team loses, he gets mad enough to FRACTURE US.

Fraternize (verb): to be friendly with. 2

Think: FRAT.

We FRAT brothers FRATERNIZE with all the freshman chicks so they'll come to our parties.

Frenetic (adjective): wildly excited or active. 2

Think: FRENZY of ENERGY.

Have you ever watched a pug play? It's FRENETIC - like a chubby little FRENZY of ENERGY.

Froward (adjective): stubbornly disobedient. 3

Think: AFRO.

I try to straighten my hair but it's FROWARD - after a few hours, it's a FRO again.

Frugal (adjective): thrifty; inclined to save money. 1

Think: FRUCTOSE corn syrup GAL.

I'm too FRUGAL to use healthy sweeteners - I'm a high-FRUCTOSE corn syrup GAL.

Fruition (noun): a productive result. 2

Think: grow FRUIT.

My plans to grow my own oranges came to FRUITION when my orange tree produced FRUIT.

Fudge (verb): to fake or falsify. 2

Think: "OH, FUDGE!"

If the salesperson FUDGES the facts about the used car you buy, you'll be saying "OH, FUDGE!" later when it breaks down.

Fuliginous (adjective): obscure; murky; dark. 3

Think: FULL OF GIN.

After he was FULL OF GIN, James Joyce composed poetry so moody and FULIGINOUS that few could appreciate it.

Fulsome (adjective): abundant, sometimes disgustingly so. 2

Think: FULL of SOME.

In the U.S., we are FULL of SOME crops - for instance, corn here is so FULSOME that we put it in nearly every food product.

Funereal (adjective): like a funeral. 2

Think: FUNERAL.

Your gothic style is so FUNEREAL it looks as though you're headed to a FUNERAL instead of the mall.

Furor (noun): an outburst of rage or excitement. 2

Think: FURIOUS.

The governor's use of the Fuhrer's (Hitler's) image in an ad made many FURIOUS and created a political FUROR.

Furtive (adjective): done by stealth. 2

Think: FURTIVE FART.

Watch out for that kid - he will FART in class but it's so FURTIVE that he never gets blamed.

Gaffe (noun): a social mistake. 2

Think: LAUGH.

It's definitely a GAFFE to bring your pet giraffe to the party - everyone will LAUGH.

Gainsay (verb): to deny. 2

Think: AGAINST SAY.

Those who GAINSAY us are AGAINST what we SAY.

Gallant (adjective): courageous; noble. 2

Think: GALLOPING knight.

She's still single because she's waiting for a GALLANT knight to come GALLOPING in on his horse and sweep her away.

Gambit (noun): a move made to try to gain an advantage. 2

Think: GAMBLE IT.

When you play chess, sometimes you have to GAMBLE IT and use a GAMBIT by sacrificing a piece for a better position.

Gamboled (verb): danced around happily; frolicked. 3

Think: GAME BALL.

After she scored three goals and led the team to victory, the coach awarded her the GAME BALL and she GAMBOLED all over the place.

Garble (verb): to make hard to understand. 2

Think: GARGLE.

A bad connection can GARBLE a voicemail to the point that the message just sounds like someone mid-GARGLE.

Gargantuan (adjective): enormous. 2

Think: GIGANTIC.

The GARGANTUAN orangutan was so GIGANTIC that it needed a special enclosure at the zoo.

Garrulous (adjective): annoyingly talkative. 2

Think: GORILLAZ.

The rapper in the band GORILLAZ is GARRULOUS, especially since he uses phrases like "chocolate attack".

Gauche (adjective): awkward. 2

Think: GO DOUCHE.

The GAUCHE thing about Summer's Eve commercials is that they're basically telling you to GO DOUCHE.

Gaudy (adjective): flashy in a tasteless way. 1

Think: GAWD UGLY.

The rapper's inch-thick gold chain was so GAUDY that even his fans said, "GAWD that's UGLY!"

Genial (adjective): good-natured. 2

Think: GENIE.

If you sign up to be a GENIE and to grant people wishes, you're probably by nature GENIAL.

Germinate (verb): to grow or to cause to grow. 2

Think: GERM IN NATE.

After entering his nose, the GERM IN NATE was able to GERMINATE into a cold because he was so run down.

Glacial (adjective): slow and/or cold. 2

Think: GLACIER.

My answer had a GLACIAL (slow) pace, and the interviewer gave me a GLACIAL (cold) look that made me feel like I was on a GLACIER.

Glancing (adjective): indirect. 2

Think: GLANCE (verb).

The knight only GLANCED sideways at his opponent; as a result, his lance's blow was GLANCING and didn't inflict any damage.

Glowered (verb): looked at with anger. 2

Think: GLOW RRR.

The scary, frowning jack-o'-lantern GLOWERED at us - its GLOW seemed to say "RRRRRRRR!"

Glut (noun): too much of something. 2

Think: GLUTTON.

Since my dog is a GLUTTON for dog treats, I have a GLUT of Snausages in my house.

Gossamer (adjective): delicate; flimsy. 2

Think: GOOSE FEATHER.

Wafting through the air, the GOOSE FEATHER was GOSSAMER and felt soft to the touch when it landed on my palm.

Grandiloquent (adjective): loud; colorful; egotistical. 3

Think: GRAND ELOQUENT.

If you're GRANDILOQUENT, you're GRAND and ELOQUENT with your speech so everyone notices you.

Grandiose (adjective): affecting grandness by showing off or exaggerating. 2

Think: GRAND IDEAS.

I have a lot of GRAND IDEAS: for example, my GRANDIOSE plan to jump the Grand Canyon with my rocket car.

Grandstand (verb): to show off. 2

Think: HANDSTAND.

If you're doing a HANDSTAND, it's probably to GRANDSTAND for an audience.

Grasping (adjective): excessively greedy. 2

Think: Mr. Burns' GRASPING.

The Simpsons' Mr. Burns is a GRASPING (adjective) tycoon who is always GRASPING (verb) at any new source of profit.

Grating (adjective): irritating. 2

Think: GRATER.

Reading Facebook election posts is GRATING; I'd almost rather rub a cheese GRATER on myself.

Gravitas (noun): powerful seriousness. 2

Think: GRAVITY.

As the judge entered, his GRAVITAS was like GRAVITY, drawing everyone's eyes to him and silencing the room.

Gregarious (adjective): social. 2

Think: CONGREGATE.

If you're GREGARIOUS, you like to CONGREGATE with others whenever possible.

Grisly (adjective): horrific; disgusting. 1

Think: GRIZZLY death.

If you piss off a GRIZZLY bear, it may give you a GRISLY death.

Grouse (verb): to complain. 2

Think: GROUCH.

Oscar the GROUCH likes to GROUSE about everyone else on Sesame Street.

Grovel (verb): to act like an unworthy servant by crawling or lowering oneself. 2

Think: GRAVEL.

GROVEL to her majesty by putting your face in the GRAVEL, slave!

Gumption (noun): drive; initiative. 2

Think: Forrest GUMP.

Forrest GUMP showed GUMPTION by playing football, co-founding a shrimp business, and running across the country.

Guttural (adjective): strange and unpleasant sounding. 2

Think: GUTTER ROAR.

You'd have the GUTTURAL GUTTER ROAR of a homeless man if you spent the night sleeping in the gutter.

Hackneyed (adjective): trite or overused. 2

Think: HACKED KNEES.

The veteran soccer player had HACKED KNEES; his knees were HACKNEYED from overuse.

Haggard (adjective): worn-out looking. 2

Think: HAG.

After months of partying with little sleep, Lindsay Lohan began to look HAGGARD and worried people would think she was an old HAG.

Halcyon (adjective): happy; peaceful; prosperous. 2

Think: HELL'S SHE ON?

In her HALCYON years, people would ask "What the HELL'S SHE ON?" because she was constantly happy.

Hallowed (adjective): sacred. 2

Think: HALO-ED.

The cemetery where saints are buried is so HALLOWED it's practically "HALO-ED".

Hapless (adjective): unlucky. 2

Think: HAPPY LESS.

The HAPLESS are often HAPPY LESS because of their rotten luck.

Harangue (noun): a ranting lecture. 2

Think: HER EARS RANG.

HER EARS RANG so much after the loud HARANGUE that she joked she'd rather hang than listen to it again.

Harbinger (noun): something that shows what will happen in the future. 2

Think: BRINGER.

The superstitious woman thought the black cat crossing her path was a HARBINGER of bad luck and a BRINGER of misfortune.

Harried (adjective): harassed. 2

Think: HURRIED.

Being HARRIED by your teacher and HURRIED to finish your test - just because you're the last one in the room - is terrible.

Harrow (verb): to torment or greatly distress. 3

Think: HAIR ARROW.

Not two days after I'd grown the perfect afro, my friend decided to HARROW me by shooting me in the HAIR with an ARROW.

Haughty (adjective): proud in a way that looks down on others. 1

Think: stuck-up HOTTIE.

Unfortunately, that senior class HOTTIE is usually HAUGHTY when you talk to her.

Headlong (adjective): done without adequate thinking; rash. 1

Think: HEADFIRST.

If you dived HEADFIRST into a shallow pool, it would be a HEADLONG decision.

Hector (verb): to bully or harass. 3

Think: HECKLE.

I tried to HECTOR the comedian by HECKLING him, but he made fun of me, so I stopped.

Hegemony (noun): dominance. 3

Think: HUGE MONEY.

The country with HUGE amounts of MONEY enjoyed HEGEMONY over its neighbors because it could afford an immense army.

Heinous (adjective): wicked; hateable. 1

Think: ANUS.

I called you an ANUS because of your HEINOUS deeds – you cheated on me!

Hermetic (adjective): protected from outside influence. 2

Think: HERMIT.

The HERMIT lived in a HERMETIC cave that was only reachable via a treacherous mountain path.

Heterogeneous (adjective): made of dissimilar parts. 2

Think: HETEROSEXUAL.

HETEROSEXUAL sex is more HETEROGENEOUS than homosexual sex since it involves a wider variety of body parts.

Heyday (noun): one's best time period. 2

Think: HEY DAY.

During my HEYDAY, when I was the starting quarterback and had a 4.0, all the girls said HEY to me every DAY.

Hiatus (noun): an interruption or break. 2

Think: HYATT.

The Hawaiian HYATT ad urged us to take a HIATUS from work to stay at its luxurious hotel for a few days.

Hidebound (adjective): inflexible; ultra-conservative. 3

Think: HIDE-BOUND.

The HIDEBOUND extremists were BOUND in animal HIDES and unsurprisingly were against gay marriage.

Hirsute (adjective): hairy. 2

Think: HAIR SUIT.

I saw an old guy in the locker room who was so HIRSUTE that he looked like he was wearing a HAIR SUIT.

Histrionic (adjective): overly emotional for effect. 2

Think: HYSTERICAL.

Her HYSTERICAL laughter was designed to get attention and was therefore HISTRIONIC.

Holistic (adjective): dealing with something as a whole. 1

Think: WHOLE LIST.

HOLISTIC medicine treats the WHOLE LIST of body issues instead of just addressing one symptom.

Homespun (adjective): simple; unpretentious. 2

Think: HOME SPUN.

Her clothes are pretty HOMESPUN, but then again, they actually *are* HOME SPUN - her mom weaves them at home on a loom.

Homogeneous (adjective): having the same composition throughout. 2

Think: HOMOGENIZED milk.

Milk is HOMOGENIZED to mix in the cream and make a HOMOGENEOUS liquid.

Hubris (noun): excessive pride or self-confidence. 2

Think: HUGE BREASTS.

If a girl gets implants and suddenly has HUGE BREASTS, she may develop HUBRIS from all the male attention.

Humbuggery (noun): nonsense; rubbish. 2

Think: BAH, HUMBUG!

Ebenezer Scrooge said, "BAH, HUMBUG!" so much because he thought Christmas was HUMBUGGERY.

Humdrum (adjective): boring. 2

Think: HUMS and DRUMS.

That was a HUMDRUM band – it was just one guy who would HUM and another guy beating a DRUM.

Husbandry (noun): careful management. 3

Think: HUSBAND.

In the 1950s, a woman's HUSBAND usually practiced HUSBANDRY of their finances.

Iconoclast (noun): someone who goes against society. 2

Think: CLASHED.

The ICONOCLAST had beliefs that CLASHED with most people's views.

Idyllic (adjective): pleasingly, naturally simple. 2

Think: IDEAL.

The IDYLLIC forest grove, with its sunbeams, babbling brook, and butterflies, seemed an IDEAL campsite.

Idiosyncrasy (noun): a weird trait. 2

Think: 'N SYNC-CRACY.

I might seem idiotic to suggest an 'N SYNC-CRACY where 'N SYNC rules our nation, but it's just my IDIOSYNCRASY.

Ignominy (noun): deep disgrace. 3

Think: IGNORED MANY.

Joe Paterno IGNORED MANY of the crimes that were being committed at Penn State; his legacy is now one of IGNOMINY.

Illiberal (adjective): narrow-minded. 2

Think: ILL LIBERAL.

Unlike his fellow open-minded Democrats, Jack was so ILLIBERAL that people thought he must be a mentally ILL LIBERAL.

Illusory (adjective): not real. 1

Think: ILLUSION.

The mirage of an oasis in the desert was an ILLUSION; it was therefore ILLUSORY.

Imbroglio (noun): complicated situation. 3

Think: IGLOO BRO.

I knew my friend was in an IMBROGLIO after getting the text, "I just woke up and I'M IN AN IGLOO, BRO!"

Imminent (adjective): about to happen. 1

Think: IN A MOMENT.

The evil-looking storm clouds told us a downpour was IMMINENT – it would happen IN A MOMENT.

Immutable (noun): unchangeable. 1

Think: IM-MUTATE-ABLE.

They poured radioactive chemicals on me to try to make me into a mutant, but it was impossible: I'm IMMUTABLE, so I'm IM-MUTATE-ABLE.

Impassive (adjective): unemotional. 2

Think: I'M PASSIVE.

I'M PASSIVE, and I remained IMPASSIVE so the bully who stole my Dippin' Dots wouldn't hit me.

Impeccable (adjective): flawless. 1

Think: IM-PECKABLE.

Due to the IMPECCABLE net you covered my apple tree with, the crows can't get at the fruit – it's IM-PECKABLE.

Impeded (verb): blocked. 1

Think: STAMPEDE.

As I walked across the fruited plain, a buffalo STAMPEDE IMPEDED my progress.

Imperious (adjective): dominant in a kingly way. 2

Think: EMPEROR.

When we went out to dinner with the EMPEROR, he was so IMPERIOUS that he ordered all of our meals.

Impetuous (adjective): impulsive; spontaneous. 2

Think: IMPATIENT US.

IMPATIENT people like US make IMPETUOUS decisions like betting on horses with cool names without researching them first.

Impinge (verb): to trespass on one's freedoms. 2

Think: I'M PINCHED.

I'M PINCHED on the butt every time I go to that biker bar – it IMPINGES on my dignity.

Implicit (adjective): suggested but not directly expressed. 1

Think: IMPLIED.

It became IMPLICIT that the evening was over when my date IMPLIED that if she didn't leave now she would be too tired to work the next day.

Importune (verb): to nag; to persistently insist. 3

Think: "I'M POOR" TUNE.

The homeless man at the end of my block always IMPORTUNES us for money with his little "I'M POOR" TUNE.

Impregnable (adjective): unconquerable; impenetrable. 2

Think: IMPOSSIBLE to get PREGNANT.

IMPREGNABLE metal chastity belts in the Middle Ages made it IMPOSSIBLE for women who wore them to get PREGNANT.

Imprimatur (noun): official approval. 3

Think: IMPRINT.

In Game of Thrones, a king conveys his IMPRIMATUR with an IMPRINT of his crest on a scroll's wax seal.

Impromptu (adjective): without preparation. 1

Think: IMPROVISE.

If you forget your lines, I'm not going to prompt you, so just IMPROVISE and make some IMPROMPTU remarks.

Impugn (verb): to attack verbally. 2

Think: IMPLY UGLY.

Your insults IMPUGN me; they IMPLY UGLY things.

Inane (adjective): lacking meaning; silly. 2

Think: INSANE.

Saying you "like stuff" to describe your interests is INANE, and it might make people think you're INSANE.

Incandescent (adjective): bright; brilliant. 2

Think: CANDLE SENT.

The CANDLE SENT INCANDESCENT light throughout the tomb, revealing a sleeping vampire.

Incensed (adjective): extremely angry. 2

Think: INCENSE.

If you're INCENSED, smoke may be wafting off of your head as if you were a giant stick of burning INCENSE (noun).

Inchoate (adjective): incomplete; formless. 3

Think: INCHES OF CHOW.

The pile of CHOW on the hungry man's Thanksgiving dinner place was eight INCHES high -- and created an INCHOATE blob of food.

Incisive (adjective): sharp; direct. 2

Think: INCISION.

Luckily, the surgeon was INCISIVE - she only had seconds to make an INCISION before the patient's appendix burst.

Incoherent (adjective): unclear. 2

Think: I COULDN'T HEAR IT.

Your slurred voicemail to me at 2:30 A.M. was INCOHERENT - I COULDN'T HEAR IT.

Incorrigible (adjective): unable to be reformed. 2

Think: IN-CORRECTABLE.

Despite his teachers' best efforts to make him sit still, the hyperactive little boy seemed INCORRIGIBLE and IN-CORRECTABLE.

Inculcate (verb): to teach by constant repetition and warning. 3

Think: IN CULT.

IN the CULT of Scientology, they INCULCATED Tom Cruise until he was brainwashed.

Indigenous (adjective): native to an area. 2

Think: INDIAN DIG IN U.S.

The archaeologist found arrowheads during her INDIAN DIG IN THE U.S. and concluded that Native Americans were INDIGENOUS to the area.

Indomitable (adjective): unconquerable. 2

Think: IN-DOMINATE-ABLE.

Spain's national soccer team is so good that they're INDOMITABLE or "IN-DOMINATE-ABLE" - they're unable to be dominated.

Industrious (adjective): hard-working. 2

Think: Maids DUSTING.

Succeeding in the cleaning industry means only hiring INDUSTRIOUS maids who are really good at DUSTING.

Ineffable (adjective): that which cannot be described in words. 2

Think: IN-F-ABLE.

There's a word beginning with "F" that you're not supposed to say, so if you can't describe something, it's INEFFABLE - like that word is "IN-F-ABLE".

Ineluctable (adjective): inevitable, bound to happen, certain. 3

Think: UNELECTABLE.

It is INELUCTABLE that a sex scandal on the eve of the election would render the candidate UNELECTABLE.

Inexorable (adjective): unstoppable. 2

Think: IN-X-OUT-ABLE.

The fighter's INEXORABLE rise made it impossible to cross his name off the contender list; he was "IN-X-OUT-ABLE".

Infinitesimal (adjective): incredibly tiny. 2

Think: INFINITELY SMALL.

Electrons are pretty much INFINITELY SMALL - they're so INFINITESIMAL that observing them changes them.

Ingenious (adjective): extremely clever. 2

Think: GENIE GENIUS.

The GENIE granted me one wish, which I used to wish for unlimited wishes. "You're a GENIUS!" he said. I know, I know.

Ingenuous (adjective): completely sincere; naive. 2

Think: GENIUS WITHOUT THE "I" IS NO GENIUS AT ALL.

The young actress, being an innocent INGENUE, was too INGENUOUS to realize the director was trying to seduce her.

Ingratiate (verb): to make someone like you. 2

Think: GRATITUDE GRATED.

The new guy's excessive GRATITUDE GRATED and seemed like an attempt to INGRATIATE himself to us.

Inimical (adjective): unfriendly; hostile. 3

Think: ENEMY.

Of course the other beauty contestant hid your lipstick! She's your ENEMY; it's no surprise she'll be INIMICAL.

Inimitable (adjective): not capable of being imitated. 2

Think: IN-IMITATE-ABLE.

Michelangelo's art is INIMITABLE and IN-IMITATE-ABLE; it has a magic that cannot be reproduced.

Innate (adjective): existing since birth; inherent. 2

Think: IN NATAL.

The ability of a spider to spin a web is not learned but INNATE; it's IN IT even in the NATAL stage before being born.

Innocuous (adjective): harmless. 2

Think: INNOCENT.

My dog will bark at you once you come in but it's INNOCENT - he's INNOCUOUS.

Inordinate (adjective): exceeding reasonable limits. 2

Think: NOT ORDINARY.

Joey Chestnut consumed an INORDINATE number of hot dogs; it's NOT ORDINARY that he ATE 62 of them.

Insinuate (verb): to hint or imply; to subtly introduce. 2

Think: IN SIN YOU ATE.

Pop culture INSINUATES that all women should be skinny, as if to say "IN SIN YOU ATE that piece of cake".

Insipid (adjective): bland; dull. 2

Think: IN SIPPY.

FYI: if your drinks are served IN SIPPY cups, you're probably a baby - that's why they feed you INSIPID, mushy foods.

Insular (adjective): narrow-minded. 2

Think: INSULATED.

The hermit's outlook was so INSULAR because his cave INSULATED him from the rest of the world.

Interloper (noun): one who intrudes. 2

Think: INTERRUPT ELOPE.

The INTERLOPER INTERRUPTED them from ELOPING when the priest said, "Speak now or forever hold your peace."

Intimate (verb): to hint at. 2

Think: INTIMATE apparel.

I like my girlfriend's INTIMATE (adjective) apparel because it INTIMATES (verb) at the shape of her body without looking slutty.

Intrepid (adjective): extremely brave. 2

Think: ENTRAP IT.

Instead of running from the attacking polar bear, our INTREPID guide handed us nets, shouting, "ENTRAP IT!"

Inundated (adjective): flooded. 2

Think: NUNS DATE.

After the church allowed NUNS to DATE, they INUNDATED Match.com.

Invidious (adjective): causing envy. 3

Think: ENVIOUS.

I knew marrying a supermodel would make my friends ENVIOUS – it's unfortunately an INVIDIOUS thing to do.

Inviolate (adjective): pure; intact. 2

Think: UNVIOLATED.

The virgin tract of rainforest was INVIOLATE; it had not yet been VIOLATED by greedy loggers.

Irascible (adjective): easily angered. 3

Think: IRRITABLE RASCAL.

My grandfather is an IRRITABLE old RASCAL; he's so IRASCIBLE that he yells at every waiter we ever get.

Jejune (adjective): dull; juvenile. 3

Think: JUVENILE.

My frat brothers' fart jokes are so JEJUNE that you could almost call them JUVENILE or "jejune-venile".

Jingoism (noun): extreme nationalism, belligerent foreign policy. 3

Think: RINGO-ISM.

The British man's JINGOISM went so far as to make him campaign for the Beatles' RINGO Starr to rule the free world.

Jocose (adjective): given to joking. 2

Think: JOKE COACH.

It was no surprise that the JOCOSE high school student grew up to be a JOKE COACH.

Judicious (adjective): having good judgment. 2

Think: JUDGMENT.

The Beatles' song "Hey JUDE" says to be JUDICIOUS, to use good JUDGMENT, and to "let her into your heart".

Juggernaut (noun): something very powerful. 2

Think: JUGGLER-KNOT.

That JUGGLER tied that huge KNOT by juggling six balls of yarn - it'll be a JUGGERNAUT to untie.

Juvenescence (noun): the state of being youthful or growing young. 3

Think: JUVENILE ADOLESCENT.

Creating JUVENESCENCE by partying in Vegas for his 40th birthday made the man feel like a JUVENILE ADOLESCENT again.

Kindle (verb): to start; to stir up. 2

Think: KINDLING.

You can't just light a log on fire - to KINDLE the campfire, you need some KINDLING: twigs, paper, dried grass, etc.

Kismet (noun): fate. 2

Think: KISS MET.

I knew it was KISMET that I'd marry her because we KISSED as soon as we MET each other.

Kowtow (verb): to kiss up to. 2

Think: COW TOES.

If you want to KOWTOW to a farmer, BOW and offer to give a pedicure to his COW's TOEs.

Lachrymose (adjective): tearful; mournful. 3

Think: LACK CHRISTMAS.

If you LACK CHRISTMAS presents, I don't blame you for being LACHRYMOSE.

Lackadaisical (adjective): without energy or spirit. 2

Think: LIKE A DAZE.

LACKADAISICAL people are lazy, LIKE a DAZE has come over them.

Laconic (adjective): using few words. 2

Think: LACKING KICK.

His personality was LACKING KICK; he was so LACONIC that barely even said hello to us.

Languid (adjective): lazy; lacking energy. 2

Think: LAYING SQUID.

The LAYING SQUID was LANGUID because it just lay on the bottom of the ocean all day.

Largess (noun): generosity. 2

Think: LARGE-NESS.

Due to his wealthy parents' LARGESS and the LARGE-NESS of their generosity, the college student lived pretty large and drove a Ferrari.

Lassitude (noun): tiredness; laziness. 2

Think: LAZY ATTITUDE.

Your LASSITUDE is caused by your LAZY ATTITUDE and your belief that Lassie will come save you if you need help.

Latent (adjective): existing but unseen or inactive. 1

Think: LAY TENT.

You claim to like hiking, but your desire must be LATENT since you just LAY in the TENT when we camp.

Laudable (adjective): worthy of praise. 2

Think: APPLAUDABLE.

Something that's LAUDABLE is APPLAUDABLE.

Lax (adjective): loose; not strict. 2

Think: LACKS.

His diet plan was LAX because he LACKS the discipline to avoid junk food.

Legerdemain (noun): sleight of hand; a display of skill. 3

Think: LEDGER'S DOMAIN.

Heath LEDGER's DOMAIN was the silver screen; his acting LEGERDEMAIN captivated audiences.

Levity (noun): lightheartedness. 2

Think: LEVITATE.

The comedian's LEVITY put us in such a good mood that our spirits felt as if they were LEVITATING.

Licentious (adjective): lacking restraint. 2

Think: LICENSE-ish.

Flappers were thought to be LICENTIOUS, since they acted as if they had a LICENSE to do whatever they wanted.

Lionized (verb): treated with great interest. 2

Think: LION-IZED.

The cute little meerkat was so LIONIZED by the zoo's visitors that he felt like a LION.

Listless (adjective): having little interest or energy. 2

Think: LIST-LESS.

If you've never made a to-do LIST, you're LIST-LESS and probably LISTLESS.

Logorrhea (noun): excessive wordiness. 3

Think: DIARRHEA.

I thought a long speech would help my grade, but my teacher said my LOGORRHEA was like verbal DIARRHEA.

Loquacious (adjective): very talkative. 2

Think: QUACK QUACK.

The LOQUACIOUS duck just wouldn't shut up: "QUACK QUACK, I'm a duck, QUACK QUACK, blah blah blah."

Lovelorn (adjective): without love. 2

Think: LOVE TORN.

After his wife died in an accident, the man felt LOVELORN, as though he'd had his LOVE TORN from him.

Lucre (noun): money; profit. 2

Think: LUCRATIVE.

When you put in the years of training necessary to secure a LUCRATIVE career, LUCRE is your reward.

Ludicrous (adjective): ridiculous. 2

Think: LUDACRIS RIDICULOUS.

The rapper LUDACRIS is known for his RIDICULOUS, LUDICROUS lines like "I got hoes in different area codes."

Lugubrious (adjective): mournful or gloomy. 3

Think: LUG BRIAN.

I became LUGUBRIOUS when I realized I would have to LUG the unconscious BRIAN up the stairs.

Lumber (verb): to move with clumsiness. 1

Think: LUMBER (noun).

Frankenstein would LUMBER (verb) around as if his limbs were made of LUMBER (noun).

Luminary (noun): one regarded for his brilliant achievements. 2

Think: ILLUMINATE.

It would take a LUMINARY like Stephen Hawking to ILLUMINATE quantum physics for me.

Lurid (adjective): sensational; shocking. 1

Think: LURE IN.

The strip club's LURID neon silhouette of a naked woman was designed to LURE IN lonely gentlemen.

Macabre (adjective): gruesome; horrible. 2

Think: MASSACRE.

The MASSACRE of the tourists by jungle cannibals was truly MACABRE.

Macerate (verb): to weaken, break down, or make soft. 2

Think: MACE.

Spraying a mugger in the face with MACE (tear gas) will hopefully MACERATE him.

Machination (noun): a crafty scheme. 3

Think: MACHINE NATION.

I don't trust C-3PO and R2D2; I bet they have MACHINATIONS designed to create a MACHINE NATION in which we are slaves.

Maelstrom (noun): something violently powerful; a whirlpool. 3

Think: MAIL STORM.

Spam emails flock to my inbox like a MAELSTROM; reading the MAIL STORM would suck up all my time.

Magisterial (adjective): having strong authority; kingly. 2

Think: MAJESTY.

If people are greeting you by saying "Your MAJESTY", you're probably looking MAGISTERIAL – wear that outfit again!

Magnanimous (adjective): generous. 2

Think: MAGNET for ANIMALS.

The "feed the birds" lady in *Mary Poppins* was a MAGNET for ANIMALS because she was so MAGNANIMOUS to them.

Magnate (noun): a powerful or influential person. 2

Think: chick MAGNET.

You'd be a chick MAGNET, too, if you were an oil MAGNATE like me.

Malevolent (adjective): evil. 2

Think: VIOLENT MALE.

MALEVOLENT criminals are usually VIOLENT MALES; most serial killers are men.

Malign (verb): to speak evil of. 2

Think: MALIGNANT.

The evil witch not only MALIGNED her enemies but also cast spells designed to give them MALIGNANT tumors.

Malinger (verb): to fake sickness to avoid working. 3

Think: LINGER.

Those who MALINGER often LINGER in bed, pretending to have the flu.

Malleable (adjective): able to be shaped. 2

Think: MALLET-ABLE.

24-karat gold is so MALLEABLE that you can dent it with a wooden hammer - it's "MALLET-ABLE."

Mandate (noun): an order or command. 2

Think: MANDATORY.

The captain's MANDATE was obviously MANDATORY – so swab the deck!

Manifold (adjective): diverse; varied. 2

Think: MANY FOLDS.

The surface of the brain is MANIFOLD because it has MANY FOLDS.

Marginal (adjective): very limited. 2

Think: MARGINS.

I only had MARGINAL success in deciphering the ancient manuscript because the only legible parts were the MARGINS.

Marshal (verb): to gather and organize. 2

Think: Fire MARSHAL.

The fire MARSHAL's job is to MARSHAL the volunteer firemen if there's a fire alarm.

Maudlin (adjective): overly sentimental. 2

Think: MAUDE's VIOLIN.

MAUDE played emotional VIOLIN music every time she made an entrance, so we called her MAUDLIN.

Mawkish (adjective): overly sentimental. 2

Think: MA's AWKWARD KISS.

MA is AWKWARD because she has to KISS us every time we leave the house - she's MAWKISH.

Meld (verb): to merge; to blend. 1

Think: MELT.

If your ice cream cup is half vanilla, half chocolate and it MELTS, the flavors will MELD.

Mellifluous (adjective): having a sweet, smooth, rich flow. 2

Think: MELODY FLOW.

Adele's MELLIFLUOUS voice lets a MELODY FLOW from her lips like honey.

Melodramatic (adjective): overly dramatic. 1

Think: DRAMATIC MELODY.

It's MELODRAMATIC to hire a violinist to follow you around and play a DRAMATIC MELODY when you enter a room.

Menial (adjective): a task suitable to a servant. 2

Think: ME KNEEL.

Tasks that make ME KNEEL, like scrubbing the floor, are aptly called MENIAL.

Mendicant (noun): a beggar. 3

Think: MEND? I CAN'T.

If you tell a MENDICANT to sew up the holes in his clothes, he'd probably say, "MEND? I CAN'T! They're about to fall apart."

Mephitic (adjective): foul-smelling. 4

Think: METH BREATH.

I bet the devil Mephistopheles has MEPHITIC breath, like that of a METH user.

Mercenary (adjective): motivated by money. 1

Think: MERCHANT.

I knew the MERCHANT'S compliments were insincere since he was clearly MERCENARY.

Mercurial (adjective): having rapidly changing moods. 2

Think: MERCURY.

Marie Curie was notorious for her MERCURIAL moods, which revolved as fast as the planet MERCURY.

Meretricious (adjective): falsely attractive. 3

Think: MERIT TRICKS US.

The sparkle of pyrite, or fool's gold, is MERETRICIOUS because its MERIT TRICKS US into thinking it's a precious stone.

Meshuga (adjective): foolish. 4

Think: ME SHRUGS.

As a pirate captain, ME SHRUGS at me crew when their actions be MESHUGA.

Mettle (noun): strength; stamina. 2

Think: made of METAL.

In <u>Gladiator,</u> Russell Crowe was so full of METTLE he might have been made of METAL.

Miasma (noun): an unhealthy atmosphere. 2

Think: MY ASTHMA.

The smog in Los Angeles is a MIASMA that worsens MY ASTHMA.

Microcosm (noun): a small thing representing a larger thing. 2

Think: MICRO-COSMOS.

The glow-in-the-dark stars on my ceiling are a MICROCOSM of the universe - they're a "MICRO COSMOS."

Milieu (noun): setting or environment. 2

Think: MY LOO.

I prefer to use MY LOO in my own MILIEU - other people's bathrooms are gross!

Milquetoast (noun): a timid person. 3

Think: MILHOUSE / MILKY TOAST.

MILHOUSE is a MILQUETOAST - he's about as tough as a piece of soggy, milky toast, since Bart Simpson bosses him around.

Mimetic (adjective): something that imitates or mimics. 2

Think: MIMES MIMIC.

You may think MIMES are annoying, but their MIMETIC abilities are pretty cool when they MIMIC what it would look like to be trapped in a glass box.

Minatory (adjective): threatening. 3

Think: MINOTAUR.

The MINOTAUR, a creature that is half-man and half-bull, is MINATORY by nature.

Minion (noun): a servant; a follower. 2

Think: MINI-ONE.

In <u>Austin Powers,</u> Mini-Me is Dr. Evil's MINION; he is a MINI-ONE of Dr. Evil.

Misanthrope (noun): one who hates people. 2

Think: MISTAKE to be an ANTHROPOLOGIST.

It's a huge MISTAKE to be an ANTHROPOLOGIST and study people all day long if you're a MISANTHROPE.

Miscreant (noun): a person who behaves badly or in a way that breaks the law. 2

Think: MISTAKE of CREATION.

The harsh judge believed the MISCREANT was a MISTAKE of CREATION.

Miserly (adjective): stingy or cheap with money. 1

Think: MISERABLE Scrooge.

Scrooge was MISERABLE at making friends because he was too MISERLY to ever chip in for the dinner tab.

Misnomer (noun): a wrong or inappropriate name. 2

Think: MIS-NAME.

"The Battle of Bunker Hill" is a MISNOMER: it MIS-NAMES the battle, which was actually fought on the nearby Breed's Hill.

Mitigate (verb): to lessen or make less severe. 2

Think: MITT GATE.

The thief wore oven MITTS to climb the spiked GATE of the mansion to MITIGATE the pain in his hands.

Modicum (noun): a small amount. 2

Think: MODEST AMOUNT.

My pet mouse is cheap to feed because a MODICUM, or MODEST AMOUNT, of food will fill up his little belly.

Modish (adjective): fashionable. 2

Think: MODEL-ISH.

MODISH brands like Burberry and Prada are MODEL-ISH because only models seem to actually wear them.

Monastic (adjective): strict; secluded; austere. 3

Think: MONASTERY.

If you're a MONK and you live in a MONASTERY, your life is probably MONASTIC – no partying for you.

Morass (noun): a situation that makes you stuck. 2

Think: MOLASSES.

Don't tailgate a MOLASSES truck - if you run into it and it spills on you, you'll be in a MORASS.

Mores (noun): customary rules and standards. 2

Think: MORALS.

Our society's MORES include MORALS like helping others who are less fortunate.

Moribund (adjective): dying. 3

Think: MORBID END.

If someone is MORIBUND, they're probably headed toward a MORBID END, i.e., death.

Morose: (adjective): gloomy. 2

Think: NO ROSE.

"The Bachelor" contestant was MOROSE because after the ceremony was over she still had NO ROSE.

Motile (adjective): having the ability to move. 3

Think: MOBILE.

Now that my one-year-old can walk, he's so MOTILE that I have to be really MOBILE just to catch up to him.

Motley (adjective): made up of several different parts. 2

Think: MOTLEY CRUE.

The band MOTLEY CRUE has a MOTLEY history of parties, drugs, and other types of craziness.

Mundane (adjective): commonplace. 1

Think: MONDAYS.

Asking someone if they have a "case of the MONDAYS" is such a MUNDANE saying that it's not funny anymore.

Munificent (adjective): generous or giving. 2

Think: MONEY SENT.

The MONEY SENT to us by our grandparents every year makes us consider them to be MUNIFICENT.

Myopic (adjective): shortsighted. 2

Think: MY OLD PIC.

Putting MY OLD PIC on Match.com was MYOPIC; in person, people said I was older than they'd thought I'd be.

Myriad (noun): a large number. 2

Think: MERRY ADS.

The MYRIAD of MERRY ADS during the holidays tries to persuade people to spend money on presents.

Nadir (noun): the lowest point. 2

Think: NADS.

A dude's NADS are literally the NADIR of his reproductive system.

Nascent (adjective): coming into existence; new. 2

Think: NEW CAR SCENT.

I jumped into the NASCENT BMW while it was still on the assembly line and breathed in the best NEW CAR SCENT I've ever smelled.

Nebulous (adjective): vague. 2

Think: NEBULA.

The Horsehead NEBULA is so many light-years away that we only have a NEBULOUS idea of what it's like.

Neophyte (noun): a beginner. 2

Think: NEO FIGHT.

When NEO has his first FIGHT with an agent in <u>The Matrix</u>, he is a NEOPHYTE and gets his ass kicked.

Nepotism (noun): unfairly hiring family members. 2

Think: NEPHEW FAVORITISM.

They said I practiced NEPHEW FAVORITISM and accused me of NEPOTISM when I promoted my 22-year-old nephew to vice president of the company.

Nettle (verb): to irritate. 2

Think: NEEDLE.

Poking someone with a NEEDLE is a quick way to NETTLE him.

Newfangled (adjective): new, often needlessly so. 1

Think: NEW TANGLED.

This NEWFANGLED yo-yo is so NEW to me that it's TANGLED around my entire body.

Noisome (adjective): stinky. 2

Think: NOSE POISON.

The boys' locker room is NOISOME; going in there is like taking NOSE POISON.

Non sequitur (noun): something unrelated. 2

Think: NOT SEQUENCE.

Bringing up koala bears after my girlfriend asked me about our relationship was a NON SEQUITUR; it was NOT in the right SEQUENCE.

Nondescript (adjective): plain. 2

Think: NO DESCRIPTION.

The little desert island was so NONDESCRIPT that it had NO DESCRIPTION in our guidebook.

Nonpareil (adjective): having no equal. 3

Think: NO PARALLEL.

The master parachutist had NONPAREIL skill; he truly had NO PARALLEL in the parachuting field.

Nonplussed (adjective): bewildered or confused. 3

Think: NO PLUS.

The calculator you loaned me made me NONPLUSSED during the test because it had NO PLUS button.

Nontrivial (adjective): important. 1

Think: NOT TRIVIAL.

The issue of global warming has become NONTRIVIAL; the rising of sea levels is NOT TRIVIAL.

Nostalgia (noun): a bittersweet longing for the past. 2

Think: NOSE TAMPON.

My NOSTALGIA for my glory days got so bad that I had to use a NOSE TAMPON for my constant sniffles.

Nostrum (noun): a questionable medicine or remedy. 3

Think: NOSTRIL RUM.

The Simpsons' Dr. Nick's NOSTRUM was NOSTRIL RUM - rum meant to be snorted to clear the sinuses.

Notorious (adjective): famous for being bad. 2

Think: NOTORIOUS B.I.G.

The NOTORIOUS B.I.G. got away with calling himself NOTORIOUS since he sold crack as a youth.

Novel (adjective): strikingly new. 1

Think: NOVICE.

When I was an internet NOVICE, the idea of email was NOVEL to me.

Novitiate (noun): a beginner. 4

Think: NOVICE INITIATE.

The NOVITIATE is a NOVICE frat brother, so they'll INITIATE him by making him run around campus wearing a thong.

Noxious (adjective): harmful. 1

Think: TOXIC.

Burning plastic releases NOXIOUS fumes that are TOXIC to living things.

Nuance (noun): a subtle or slight distinction. 1

Think: NEW ANTS.

Forgive me for not picking up on the NUANCE of today's experiment - I couldn't tell it had NEW ANTS compared to yesterday's - ants all look the same to me.

Nugatory (adjective): unimportant. 3

Think: Negative NUGGETS.

Eating Chicken McNUGGETS is NUGATORY for good health; their health benefits could be said to be negative.

Obdurate (adjective): hardened; stubbornly persistent. 3

Think: OBSTACLE DURABLE.

That 10-ton boulder you blocked my front door with is an OBSTACLE that's DURABLE - I tried to push it, but it's OBDURATE.

Obeisance (noun): a gesture to show respect. 3

Think: OBEY STANCE.

When the natives bowed to the conqueror in OBEISANCE, it was like an "OBEY STANCE".

Obfuscated (verb): made unclear. 2

Think: OBSTACLES CONFUSED.

The professor barely spoke English: the OBSTACLES his speech created CONFUSED us and OBFUSCATED his message.

Objective (adjective): not influenced by personal perspective. 1

Think: OBJECT.

It's easy to have an OBJECTIVE opinion about an OBJECT like a rock – there's not much debate about what a rock is.

Obstinate (adjective): stubborn. 2

Think: OBSTACLE IN IT.

The OBSTINATE horse behaved as though there was an OBSTACLE to movement IN IT.

Obstreperous (adjective): stubbornly resistant to control; noisy. 3

Think: STREP.

The bacteria that cause STREP throat are so OBSTREPEROUS that many people take antibiotics for the condition.

Occluded (adjective): closed up; blocked. 2

Think: OCTOMOM CLUTTERED.

OCTOMOM CLUTTERED the hospital's nursery with her eight babies and OCCLUDED it so no other infants were admitted.

Odious (adjective): arousing or deserving hatred. 2

Think: ODOROUS ONIONS.

Only eating onions is ODIOUS because they make one's breath so ODOROUS.

Officious (adjective): bossy. 2

Think: VICIOUS OFFICIAL.

The OFFICIAL was VICIOUS enough to measure every fish we caught with a ruler to make sure it was legal.

Omniscient (adjective): all-knowing. 2

Think: OWNS HIS SCIENCE.

I'm not surprised to hear that Jesus got an A in AP Chem; he OWNS HIS SCIENCE classes because he's OMNISCIENT.

Onus (noun): burden; obligation. 2

Think: ON US.

Since we broke the vase, the ONUS is ON US to pay for it.

Openhanded (adjective): generous. 2

Think: OPEN your HAND.

To be OPENHANDED, OPEN your HAND and share what you have with others instead of keeping it clenched in your fist.

Opine (verb): to hold or state as an opinion. 2

Think: OPINION.

If you OPINE about the election on Facebook, everyone gets to hear your OPINION whether they like it or not.

Opportune (adjective): well-timed. 2

Think: OPPORTUNITY.

It's OPPORTUNE that I got picked for this singing OPPORTUNITY because a genie just granted my wish to sing perfectly.

Opprobrium (noun): public disgrace. 3

Think: OPRAH OPPOSES.

Sometimes, OPRAH brings people she OPPOSES on her show to cause them OPPROBRIUM - it's like "OPRAH-BRIUM".

Ornate (adjective): elaborately or excessively decorated. 1

Think: ORNAMENTS.

ORNAMENTS covered every inch of the Christmas tree due to the decorator's ORNATE style.

Orthodox (adjective): conventional; traditional. 2

Think: ORTHODONTIST.

Look for an ORTHODOX ORTHODONTIST; you don't want someone getting creative with your teeth.

Ossified (verb): became hard or inflexible. 2

Think: FOSSIL-FIED.

The Velociraptor's bones could bend slightly, but after death, they OSSIFIED and turned into FOSSILS.

Ostentatious (adjective): showy; pretentious; boastful. 2

Think: OSTRICH STUNT.

That OSTRICH STUNT - when you showed up at the prom riding one like a horse - was OSTENTATIOUS.

Ostracized (verb): excluded. 2

Think: OSTRICH-SIZED.

That poor kid is OSTRICH-SIZED – he'll be OSTRACIZED as soon as he starts high school.

Otiose (adjective): useless; lazy. 4

Think: TORTOISE fetch.

Playing fetch with this TORTOISE is OTIOSE.

Outstrip (verb): to outrun or to exceed. 2

Think: OUT-STRIP.

To be fair, that STRIPPER gets more tips than you because her pole-dancing skills OUTSTRIP yours.

Overweening (adjective): arrogant. 2

Think: WEENIE.

The young actor's demands were so OVERWEENING that the movie crew started calling him a WEENIE behind his back.

Pacific (adjective): soothing. 2

Think: PACIFIER.

The infant's PACIFIER had a PACIFIC effect, and she was soon asleep.

Painstaking (adjective): very careful. 1

Think: TAKING PAINS.

TAKING PAINS to not infect the patient means being PAINSTAKING when you wash your hands before surgery.

Palatable (adjective): tasty. 2

Think: PAL AT TABLE.

Having my PAL AT the TABLE for dinner seems to make the food more PALATABLE since I'm in a good mood.

Palatial (adjective): magnificent. 1

Think: PALACE.

The PALATIAL resort, with luxurious amenities and gourmet food, was like a PALACE.

Palliate (verb): to reduce the severity of. 2

Think: PILL I ATE.

The prescription PILL I ATE should PALLIATE my depression.

Pallid (adjective): lacking color. 2

Think: PALE.

After playing video games in his mother's basement all winter, Al was so PALE his friends described him as PALLID.

Panacea (noun): a cure-all. 2

Think: PAN OF Vitamin C.

The hippie advised me that eating a PAN OF vitamin C is a PANACEA for illness.

Pander: (verb): to appeal to someone's desire for selfish reasons. 2

Think: PANDA logo.

The American company that used a PANDA as its logo was accused of PANDERING to the Chinese market.

Pangs (noun): sharp feelings of pain. 2

Think: PAINS.

I read *The Hunger Games* for six hours, but then had to stop because of the PAINS from my own hunger PANGS.

Paradigm (noun): an example used as a pattern or model.

Think: PAIR OF DIMES.

Those two girls are a PAIR OF DIMES since they're both 10s – they're PARADIGMS for how to look hot.

Paragon (noun): a model of excellence. 2

Think: ARAGORN.

If you're looking for a PARAGON in <u>The Lord of the Rings</u>, choose ARAGORN: he became the king.

Pariah (noun): an outcast. 2

Think: MARIAH'S anthem.

MARIAH Carey became a PARIAH after butchering the national anthem in front of 80,000 fans.

Parley (verb): to talk. 2

Think: PARSLEY.

If you're going to PARLEY with someone you like, eat some PARSLEY - it's good for your breath.

Parochial (adjective): narrow-minded. 2

Think: PARISH YOKEL.

Our church is led by a PARISH YOKEL who is so PAROCHIAL that he believes women should be barefoot and pregnant.

Parody (noun): a mocking or satirical imitation. 1

Think: PARROT-Y.

Pro tip: a good way to make fun of someone is to repeat what he just said in a squawky PARROT-Y voice, to PARODY him.

Paroxysm: (noun): an attack, spasm, or outburst. 3

Think: PARADOX SPASM.

If you drink ocean water, you'll have a PAROXYSM – it's a PARADOX that it's water but it causes SPASMS if you swallow it.

Parsimonious (adjective): stingy. 2

Think: PARSLEY MONEY.

My dad was so PARSIMONIOUS he'd give us PARSLEY MONEY instead of lunch money.

Partisan (adjective): biased toward one side. 2

Think: PARTY'S SON.

The chairman of the Democratic PARTY'S SON was understandably PARTISAN about politics.

Pastiche (noun): an imitation; something made of many things. 3

Think: PASTE EACH.

If you copy Wikipedia and PASTE EACH entry into your paper, it will be a PASTICHE.

Pathos (noun): a quality that evokes feelings of sadness or pity. 2

Think: SYMPATHY OHHHS.

Your painting of a starving puppy has so much PATHOS that it always gets SYMPATHY "OHHHS" from viewers.

Patois (noun): the speech/slang used by a certain group. 3

Think: PATIO SPEECH.

PATIO SPEECH during barbecues is more likely to contain PATOIS than speech in the office.

Paucity (noun): lack of. 2

Think: POOR CITY.

In the POOR CITY, there was a PAUCITY of resources.

Pedestrian (adjective): dull; ordinary. 2

Think: PEDESTRIAN (noun).

You're PEDESTRIAN (adjective) because you're a PEDESTRIAN (noun) – cool kids drive to school.

Peevish (adjective): irritable; whiny; bratty. 2

Think: PET PEEVE.

In the *Harry Potter* books, Peeves is a PEEVISH ghost in Hogwarts whose PET PEEVE is happy students - so he tattletales on them.

Penchant (noun): a liking for something. 2

Think: PENDANT ENCHANT.

If a girl wears a low hanging PENDANT to ENCHANT the boys, they'll soon have a PENCHANT for her.

Pendulous (adjective): hanging loosely; sagging. 2

Think: PENDULUM.

As the naked old lady danced, her PENDULOUS breasts swung back and forth like the PENDULUMS of grandfather clocks.

Penitent (adjective): being sorry for one's actions. 2

Think: REPENT.

The beggar's sign read, "REPENT! Do penance for your sins! Only the PENITENT will see God!"

Penurious (adjective): stingy. 3

Think: PENNY FURIOUS.

The PENNY tip made the waiter FURIOUS; the customer must have been PENURIOUS.

Penury (noun): severe poverty. 3

Think: PENALTY.

The court's PENALTY was so large that the defendant suffered from PENURY to the point of only owning one penny.

Peons (noun): lower-class workers used by someone of a superior class. 2

Think: PEE-ONS.

The nobleman so little respected his PEONS that he would PEE ON them.

Peregrinate (verb): to journey or travel from place to place. 3

Think: PEREGRIN Falcon.

The fastest member of the animal kingdom is the PEREGRIN Falcon; it exceeds 200 m.p.h. while diving and can PEREGRINATE speedily.

Peremptory (adjective): bossy, prone to cutting others off. 3

Think: PRE-EMPTED.

The Emperor PRE-EMPTED Luke's replies so much that even Darth Vader called him PEREMPTORY.

Perennial (adjective): constant; persistent; recurring. 2

Think: PER ANNUAL.

PER the ANNUAL tradition, it's time to start the PERENNIAL search for the next American Idol.

Perfidy (noun): treachery; treason. 3

Think: PERFORATED FIDELITY.

When I realized my friend spread rumors about me, I felt like he had PERFORATED FIDELITY because of his PERFIDY.

Perfunctory (adjective): showing little interest. 2

Think: PER FUNCTION problem.

I know I won't get them right, so I only spend a PERFUNCTORY amount of time PER FUNCTION problem.

Peripatetic (adjective): wandering; traveling; constantly moving from place to place. 3

Think: PITTER-PATTER.

The mouse in my house is PERIPATETIC since I'm constantly hearing the PITTER-PATTER of his little feet in the walls.

Permeated (verb): spread through; penetrated. 2

Think: PERM HE ATE.

The PERM HE ATE will PERMEATE his stomach lining and prove it's stupid to eat human hair.

Permutation (noun): a transformation or rearrangement. 2

Think: MUTATION.

A radioactive spider bite caused a PERMUTATION of Peter Parker's genes and caused his MUTATION into Spiderman.

Pernicious (adjective): destructive; deadly. 3

Think: PIRANHAS VICIOUS.

PIRANHAS are VICIOUS; lingering in waters they inhabit can be PERNICIOUS.

Perquisites (noun): privileges or bonuses. 3

Think: PERKS.

Hey suckahhhs - now that I'm CEO, I enjoy
PERQUISITES like a company helicopter and a gold
wastebasket - PERKS you'll never have.

Perspicacious (adjective): sharp; clever. 3

Think: PERSPECTIVE for the ACES.

A PERSPICACIOUS poker player uses her clear
PERSPECTIVE to know who has the ACES.

Pertinacious (adjective): stubbornly persistent. 3

Think: PERSISTENT and TENACIOUS.

My PERTINACIOUS defender was both PERSISTENT
and TENACIOUS; I had no open shots.

Perturb (verb): to disturb greatly. 2

Think: DISTURBED by TURDS.

The TURDS your dog leaves on my beautiful lawn not only
DISTURB me - they PERTURB me.

Perverse (adjective): bad; wrong; corrupt. 1

Think: PERVERTS.

PERVERTS like peeping toms are PERVERSE; they should be locked up.

Petulant (adjective): rude; irritable. 2

Think: PETTY AUNT.

My PETTY AUNT is always whining about something or holding a grudge; she's PETULANT.

Philander (verb): to have casual or unfaithful sex. 4

Think: ZOOLANDER.

When you're ridiculously good-looking like ZOOLANDER, it's easy to PHILANDER.

Phlegmatic (adjective): sluggish; unresponsive. 3

Think: PHLEGM.

When I had the flu, I had so much PHLEGM clogging my respiratory system that I was completely PHLEGMATIC.

Physiological (adjective): related to the body. 1

Think: PHYSICAL.

I knew I wasn't just imagining I was ill because my PHYSIOLOGICAL symptom, a fever of 103, was PHYSICAL.

Picaresque (adjective): about someone's adventures. 3

Think: PIXAR-ESQUE.

Your novel is like <u>Wall-E</u> because of your hero's journey; it's both PICARESQUE and PIXAR-ESQUE.

Picayune (adjective): unimportant; small-minded. 3

Think: PICKY ONE.

The PICAYUNE bridezilla was quite the PICKY ONE, worrying about every single detail of her wedding.

Picturesque (adjective): lovely. 2

Think: PICTURES.

The Grand Canyon at sunrise is so PICTURESQUE that you can't help but take PICTURES.

Piebald (adjective): many-colored; varied. 3

Think: PIES.

The horse's coat was PIEBALD, pebbled with blotches of so many colors that it looked like PIES were thrown at it.

Piquant (adjective): pleasantly spicy or tangy. 2

Think: PICKLED ANT.

I never thought I'd like eating PICKLED ANT, but it's surprisingly PIQUANT.

Pith (noun): the essential or central part. 2

Think: PIT.

If you're a peach tree, the PITH of your fruit is the PIT, since that's how you'll reproduce.

Pittance (noun): a very small amount. 2

Think: PIT ANTS.

PIT ANTS are known for eating even the PITTANCE of fruit that clings to discarded peach pits.

Plaintive (adjective): melancholy. 2

Think: COMPLAINT.

When I hear the PLAINTIVE cry of a seagull, it always sounds like a COMPLAINT about the bird's woes or travails.

Platitude (noun): an overused expression. 2

Think: BLAH ATTITUDE.

Dude, she's giving you that BLAH ATTITUDE cause your pickup line was a PLATITUDE.

Platonic (adjective): not related to romance or sex. 2

Think: PLATO DATE.

If you only talk to your date about the philosopher PLATO, you'll end up as her PLATONIC friend.

Plaudits (noun): approval. 2

Think: APPLAUD IT.

If you want to give PLAUDITS to his work, APPLAUD IT.

Plausible (adjective): apparently true. 1

Think: APPLAUSE-ABLE.

When the magician sawed the lady in half, it looked so PLAUSIBLE that it was APPLAUSE-ABLE.

Plebeian (adjective): common; low-class. 2

Think: FLEAS BE IN.

I don't stay in PLEBEIAN motels 'cause FLEAS BE IN 'em.

Plenipotentiary (adjective): fully empowered. 3

Think: PLENTY of POTENCY.

If Romney wins the election, he will be PLENIPOTENTIARY; being president will give him PLENTY of POTENCY.

Pluck (noun): courage; spirit. 2

Think: PLUCK a feather.

You showed PLUCK by attempting to PLUCK a feather from a live ostrich; too bad it decided to peck you in the eye.

Plutocracy (noun): government controlled by the wealthy. 2

Think: PLUTO vacation home.

Hearing about the senator's vacation home on PLUTO made me realize we're in a PLUTOCRACY.

Polarize (verb): to separate into two conflicting or opposite positions. 2

Think: Earth's POLES.

Democrats and Republicans are so POLARIZED that I'm surprised they don't stay at the North and South POLES to keep as far apart as they can.

Polemic (noun): a harsh attack against a principle. 3

Think: POLITICIAN at a MIC.

Put a POLITICIAN at a MIC, and you'll soon hear POLEMIC as he attacks his opponent's policies.

Politesse (noun): politeness. 2

Think: POLITENESS.

French maids are trained to show POLITENESS at all times; their POLITESSE is without equal.

Politic (adjective): shrewd; wise. 2

Think: POLITICIAN.

After reading *The Prince* by Machiavelli, the POLITICIAN became much more POLITIC and cleverly defeated his opponent.

Ponderous (adjective): heavy; dull. 1

Think: PONDER.

If a subject in school makes you PONDER it for long periods of time, it could just be that it's PONDEROUS and is either heavy, or dull, or both.

Poseur (noun): one who pretends to be something he is not. 2

Think: POSER.

The POSEUR pretended to be interested in literature to impress girls, but he was exposed as a POSER who didn't even know who Shakespeare was.

Posit (verb): to assume to be true; to suggest. 2

Think: POSITIVE.

POSITIVE about her findings, the scientist finally agreed to POSIT the existence of extraterrestrial life in a journal article.

Pragmatic (adjective): practical. 1

Think: PRACTICAL AUTOMATIC.

To be PRACTICAL, buy an AUTOMATIC car instead of a stick shift - it's more PRAGMATIC for city driving.

Prattle (noun): meaningless talk. 2

Think: baby RATTLE.

Her PRATTLE about reality TV was as exciting as listening to a baby shake its RATTLE.

Precarious (adjective): dangerously unstable. 2

Think: PREACH CAREFULNESS.

PREACH CAREFULNESS to people who are standing on PRECARIOUS rock ledges.

Precocious (adjective): very talented at a young age. 2

Think: PRE-COACHING.

Sadie was PRECOCIOUS at piano PRE-COACHING; she taught herself to play Mozart at the age of two.

Precursor (noun): something that came before another thing. 2

Think: PRE-CURSOR.

When you're typing, the word you just typed is literally PRE-CURSOR; it's before the cursor and is thus a PRECURSOR to it.

Predilection (noun): a preference. 3

Think: PREDICTED DIRECTION.

Google PREDICTED the DIRECTION of my search when I typed "how to find" by showing "how to find love", because it knows people have a PREDILECTION to seek romance.

Prescient (adjective): seeing the future; well-planned and thought out. 2

Think: knowing about PRESENT you SENT.

Since I'm PRESCIENT, I already know what's in the PRESENT you SENT me.

Pretext (noun): a fake excuse. 2

Think: PEE TEXT.

She pretends to have to PEE and leaves on the PRETEXT of using the restroom so she can TEXT without getting caught.

Prevaricate (verb): to lie. 3

Think: PREVENT VERIFY.

To cover for you, your friend will PREVARICATE and PREVENT the cop from VERIFYING what really happened.

Primordial (adjective): original; existing since the beginning. 3

Think: PRIMARY ORDER.

The Big Bang is PRIMORDIAL because it has the PRIMARY position in the ORDER of events.

Pristine (adjective): pure. 1

Think: LISTERINE.

LISTERINE mouthwash tastes bad but it kills bacteria and makes your mouth PRISTINE.

Proclivity (noun): a tendency or inclination. 2

Think: PRO-CLITORIS.

If you're PRO-CLITORIS, you probably have a PROCLIVITY to like women.

Prodigious (adjective): impressively large; extraordinary. 2

Think: PRODIGY.

The child PRODIGY could multiply PRODIGIOUS numbers in his head.

Profane (adjective): sacrilegious; vulgar; improper. 1

Think: PROFANITY.

Using PROFANITY in church is obviously PROFANE.

Profligacy (noun): reckless wastefulness. 3

Think: PROFITS FLING.

If your PROFITS FLING out the window, you're probably following a course of PROFLIGACY.

Profound (adjective): deep. 1

Think: PROFESSOR FOUND.

My PROFESSOR FOUND the cure for cancer because his decades of study gave him a PROFOUND understanding of the disease.

Profuse (adjective): plentiful; abundant. 1

Think: PROFESSORS USE.

PROFESSORS USE books with a PROFUSE amount of information to make reading assignments take forever.

Progenitors (noun): direct ancestors. 3

Think: PRODUCED from GENITALS.

You were PRODUCED from the GENITALS of your PROGENITORS.

Prognosticate (verb): to predict. 3

Think: PROFESSIONAL KNOWS.

Punxsutawney Phil, the groundhog who PROGNOSTICATES whether winter will last for six more weeks, is obviously a PROFESSIONAL that KNOWS the future.

Proliferate (verb): to grow or multiply quickly. 2

Think: PRO-LIFE-RATE.

The PRO-LIFE-RATE of births is higher than the pro-choice rate; pro-life people PROLIFERATE because they don't get abortions.

Prolific (adjective): abundantly productive. 1

Think: PRO-LIFE-IC.

That state is anti-abortion, and they're PROLIFIC baby-makers because of their PRO-LIFE-IC stance on the subject.

Prolix (adjective): too long/wordy. 3

Think: PROLIFIC.

After writing dozens of 1000+ page books, the PROLIFIC author was often criticized for his PROLIX writing style.

Prominent (adjective): well-known; standing out. 1

Think: PROM KING.

The PROM KING is usually not the shy boy that no one knows; he's often a PROMINENT, popular kid.

Promulgate (verb): to make known. 3

Think: PROMOTE MULLET.

The hillbilly hairstylist would often PROMOTE MULLETS by PROMULGATING about them to new clients.

Propensity (noun): a natural tendency. 2

Think: PRO-PENIS.

If you're a guy who is PRO-PENIS, you'll have a PROPENSITY to wear a protective cup when playing baseball.

Prophetic (adjective): that which foretells the future. 2

Think: PROPHET.

In the bible, Jesus is considered to be a PROPHET because many of his PROPHETIC claims actually happened - like predicting that Peter would deny him three times.

Propitious (adjective): favorable; promising. 3

Think: PROP IT UP.

In "A Charlie Brown Christmas", Linus thought the little tree was PROPITIOUS, so he decided to PROP IT UP.

Propriety (noun): the quality of being proper or appropriate. 2

Think: PROPER.

For the sake of PROPRIETY, use PROPER manners and eat your salad with the salad fork, not the dinner fork.

Prosaic (adjective): dull or boring. 2

Think: PROS SAY ICK.

I was going to watch the new Adam Sandler movie, but the movie critic PROS SAY, "ICK - the film is PROSAIC".

Protean (adjective): varied; versatile. 3

Think: PROTEINS.

Since they can be formed from a vast number of combinations of 500 different amino acids, PROTEINS are PROTEAN.

Provincial (adjective): narrow-minded. 2

Think: PROVINCE.

If you never leave your Canadian PROVINCE, your worldview will probably be somewhat PROVINCIAL.

Prowess (noun): exceptional bravery and/or skill. 2

Think: PROWL LIONESS.

While on the PROWL, the LIONESS displayed her PROWESS by bringing down a woolly mammoth.

Proximity (noun): closeness. 2

Think: APPROXIMATELY.

APPROXIMATELY means "close to"; PROXIMITY means closeness.

Prudent (adjective): wise. 1

Think: PRUDE STUDENT.

In high school, PRUDE STUDENTS are PRUDENT, since it's not a great idea to be 16 and pregnant.

Puerile (adjective): childish. 2

Think: PUBERTY.

The high school freshman's PUERILE sense of humor was typical of a boy who was going through PUBERTY.

Pugnacious (adjective): wanting to fight. 2

Think: PUG NATION.

Imagine how PUGNACIOUS a PUG NATION would be - those little dogs definitely would be fighting all the time.

Pulchritude (noun): beauty. 3

Think: POLL: CHRIST, DUDE.

She had so much PULCHRITUDE that the most common response about her looks in the bros' POLL was just, "CHRIST, DUDE!"

Punctilious (adjective): marked by following the rules strictly. 2

Think: PUNCTUAL.

The teacher's pet was both PUNCTILIOUS and PUNCTUAL, but most wanted to punch him.

Pungent (adjective): strongly scented. 2

Think: PUNCH SCENT.

The boxer's body odor was so PUNGENT it was like getting hit by a PUNCH of SCENT.

Punitive (adjective): involving punishment. 2

Think: PUNISH.

The PUNITIVE damages in the O.J. Simpson murder case were clearly designed to PUNISH the defendant.

Pusillanimous (adjective): cowardly. 3

Think: PUSSYCAT.

The PUSSYCAT is an animal that is PUSILLANIMOUS when scared - hence the expression "scaredy-cat".

Putrid (adjective): foul or rotten. 1

Think: PUKED.

The dead mouse smelled so PUTRID that I almost PUKED while getting rid of it.

Quagmire (noun): a difficult situation. 2

Think: QUICKSAND MIRE.

QUICKSAND can MIRE you if you step in it, and the more you struggle, the worse the QUAGMIRE becomes.

Quail (verb): to pull back in fear. 2

Think: QUAIL (the bird).

I feel bad for QUAIL (noun) - those poor birds QUAIL (verb) as soon as they see people because they're often hunted for sport.

Quash (verb): to completely stop from happening. 2

Think: SQUASH.

The best way to QUASH an invasion of ants in your kitchen is simple: SQUASH them.

Querulous (adjective): whiny; complaining. 3

Think: QUARREL US.

We'd invite you over more, but you're so QUERULOUS that you always end up in a QUARREL with US!

Quiescent (adjective): at rest. 3

Think: QUIET.

The hibernating bear was both QUIET and QUIESCENT.

Quintessential (adjective): the most typical; the purest. 3

Think: ESSENTIAL.

Watching a Red Sox game at Fenway Park is ESSENTIAL to get the QUINTESSENTIAL Boston experience.

Quixotic (adjective): idealistic; impractical. 3

Think: QUICK EXOTIC.

It's QUIXOTIC to think that you should earn some QUICK cash by becoming an EXOTIC dancer.

Quizzical (adjective): questioning; teasing. 2

Think: QUIZZING.

When I started asking my date about the periodic table, her QUIZZICAL expression seemed to be QUIZZING me about why I'd brought up such an awkward topic.

Quotidian (adjective): daily. 3

Think: QUOTA.

The meter maid met her daily QUOTA of parking tickets by her QUOTIDIAN patrolling of the streets.

Raconteur (noun): a good storyteller. 2

Think: RECOUNT.

Jack White named one of his bands The RACONTEURS because they were so good at RECOUNTING stories via song.

Ragamuffin (noun): a dirty, poor person or child. 4

Think: RAGS on MUFFIN.

The RAGS on your little MUFFIN make him look like a RAGAMUFFIN - shop at Baby Gap next time.

Raiment (noun): clothing. 2

Think: RAIN MEANT.

In the nudist colony, a forecast of RAIN MEANT they'd actually have to don some RAIMENT.

Rampant (adjective): widespread; uncontrolled. 2

Think: RAMPAGE.

If you're dumb enough to take bath salts, the destruction after your RAMPAGE will be RAMPANT.

Rancorous (adjective): hateful. 3

Think: Star Wars RANCOR.

In <u>Return Of The Jedi</u>, the RANCOR under Jabba The Hutt's palace is undoubtedly RANCOROUS for having been imprisoned.

Rankled (verb): irritated. 2

Think: WRINKLED.

Tim Gunn told the "Project Runway" contestant to "make it work", so the WRINKLED dress she made RANKLED him.

Rapacious (adjective): greedy; predatory; ravenous. 2

Think: RAPES US.

The RAPACIOUS new tax law takes so much of our earnings that it effectively RAPES US.

Rapturous (adjective): full of wonderful feelings; ecstatic. 2

Think: RAPTOR saw US.

The RAPTOR saw US being lowered into his cage and felt RAPTUROUS since he was hungry.

Rarefied (adjective): lofty; reserved only for a select few. 3

Think: RARE FIND.

The truffle your pig dug up is a RARE FIND, peasant - you dare not eat such a RAREFIED delicacy - save it for his Majesty.

Rash (adjective): hasty; incautious. 2

Think: RASH (noun).

If you make the RASH (adjective) decision to have unprotected sex with that NBA player, you might get a RASH (noun).

Raucous (adjective): noisy; disorderly. 2

Think: ROCKS US.

The Beastie Boys' RAUCOUS track, "Fight For Your Right to Party", ROCKS US.

Raze (verb): to completely destroy. 2

Think: RAYS BLAZE.

The powerful laser's RAYS are making a BLAZE that will RAZE the old building to make room for the new one.

Reap (verb): to gather or obtain. 1

Think: Grim REAPER.

If there's a knock on the door and you see the Grim REAPER through the peephole, don't answer: he has come to REAP your life.

Recalcitrant (adjective): difficult to manage or change. 3

Think: CALC RANT.

The CALC worksheet made Alex RANT because it was so RECALCITRANT.

Recant (verb): to formally deny a former position. 2

Think: REALLY I CAN'T.

I know I said I would move to Canada if we elected Obama, but REALLY I CAN'T, so I RECANT that statement.

Recapitulated (verb): summarized. 3

Think: RECAP.

His RECAP of the news nicely RECAPITULATED the day's events.

Recidivist (noun): someone who relapsed into crime. 3

Think: SID's DIVISION.

Sid had two sides to his personality: the law-abiding side and the RECIDIVIST.

Reclusive (adjective): characterized by hiding and avoiding society. 2

Think: Brown RECLUSE.

Luckily for us, the deadly poisonous Brown RECLUSE Spider is RECLUSIVE.

Recondite (adjective): not easily understood. 3

Think: RECKONED IT.

I couldn't understand my professor's RECONDITE lecture, but I RECKONED IT had something to do with the fourth dimension.

Recrudescent (adjective): reactivating. 3

Think: RECRUITS SENT.

The conflict in Afghanistan must be RECRUDESCENT since more RECRUITS are SENT there daily.

Rectitude (noun): extreme integrity. 2

Think: CORRECT ATTITUDE.

Since he was a church rector, Paul considered the CORRECT ATTITUDE to be RECTITUDE.

Redress: to set right. 2

Think: RE-DRESS Lady Gaga.

Lady Gaga's fashion choices are so wrong that the only way to REDRESS her style is to literally RE-DRESS her.

Reductive (adjective): related to making something smaller or simpler. 2

Think: REDUCE.

REDUCTIVE Spark Notes REDUCE brilliant works of literature into basic summaries.

Redundant (adjective): needlessly repetitive. 1

Think: RE-DONE.

Duh... that has already been done well - it will be REDUNDANT if you decide it needs to be REDONE.

Refracted (verb): distorted or changed from an initial direction. 2

Think: REFLECTED FRACTURED.

The prism REFRACTED the white light and REFLECTED it, FRACTURED, into a rainbow of colors.

Refractory (adjective): stubborn; unmanageable. 3

Think: RE-FRACTURE.

The REFRACTORY athlete insisted on playing despite his broken toe; unsurprisingly, he RE-FRACTURED it.

Refulgent (adjective): brightly shining. 3

Think: REFUELS IT.

The campfire gets REFULGENT after he REFUELS IT.

Rejuvenated (verb): gave new life to. 2

Think: RE-JUVENILE.

His plans for the new year REJUVENATED the middle-aged man so much that he felt like a JUVENILE again.

Relish (verb): to enjoy; to savor. 2

Think: DELISH.

I RELISH (verb) eating hot dogs with RELISH (noun) because they taste DELISH.

Remedial (adjective): intended to correct at a basic level. 2

Think: REMEDY.

If you are terrible at math, the only REMEDY might be to take a REMEDIAL arithmetic class.

Remiss (adjective): careless. 2

Think: RE-MISS.

If you are REMISS in your study technique, you'll miss the point the first time you read then RE-MISS it the 2nd time.

Remunerated (verb): compensated or paid for. 2

Think: RE-MONEYED.

It cost me $300 to remove the rat from my apartment, but my landlord REMUNERATED / "RE-MONEYED" me.

Renowned (adjective): famous in a good way. 2

Think: RE-KNOWN.

RENOWNED celebrities are often KNOWN in their era then RE-KNOWN on reality T.V. shows several years later.

Replete (adjective): full. 2

Think: REPLACE COMPLETELY.

REPLACE your energy COMPLETELY after your workout so your body stays REPLETE with energy.

Reprehensible (adjective): deserving blame. 2

Think: PRETEND HENS.

Heyyy... you sold me PRETEND HENS instead of real ones - that's REPREHENSIBLE.

Reprobate (adjective): evil. 3

Think: RE-PROBED IT.

The aliens who gave Cartman an anal probe on "South Park" would be even more REPROBATE if they RE-PROBED IT.

Repudiate (verb): to refuse to accept; to reject. 2

Think: REFUSE POO I ATE.

If I ate shit, my stomach would REFUSE the POO I ATE and REPUDIATE it by vomiting uncontrollably.

Repugnant (adjective): gross. 2

Think: UGLY PUG.

Although some people think PUGS' upturned faces and wheezing are cute, many find the breed to be REPUGNANT.

Requisite (adjective): necessary. 2

Think: REQUIRES IT.

If you fail English, your school REQUIRES IT to be re-taken; it's REQUISITE that you have four years of English.

Resigned (adjective): reluctantly accepting of a bad situation. 2

Think: RESIGNATION.

After being implicated in Watergate, Nixon was RESIGNED and offered his RESIGNATION from office.

Resolute (adjective): firmly determined. 1

Think: RESOLUTION.

It's no use to make a New Year's RESOLUTION if you're not RESOLUTE enough to follow through with it.

Respite (adjective): a short rest. 2

Think: REST IT.

Don't overwork your respiratory system; if you take a RESPITE and REST IT, your lungs will thank you.

Resplendent (adjective): shining brilliantly. 2

Think: SPLENDID.

Cinderella was RESPLENDENT in a sequined, white ball gown; she looked absolutely SPLENDID.

Restitution (noun): the act of making up for something bad. 2

Think: REST of TUITION.

My college's RESTITUTION for allowing prostitution was paying the REST of our TUITION.

Restive (adjective): restless; fidgety. 3

Think: REST on STOVE.

Good luck taking a REST on a STOVE - you'll feel too RESTIVE to sleep because you'll worry it will turn on.

Resurgence (noun): a comeback. 2

Think: RE-SURGE.

When LL Cool J said, "Don't call it a comeback", he meant that his RE-SURGING to the top wasn't a RESURGENCE.

Reticent (adjective): reserved; quiet. 2

Think: READY but HESITANT.

If you have to recite a speech and you're technically READY but HESITANT, you might be RETICENT.

Retiring (adjective): shy. 2

Think: RETIRE from parties.

The shy girl was so RETIRING that she decided that she would RETIRE from going to parties.

Retrenchment (noun): a reduction. 3

Think: RETURN to TRENCH.

For a WWI soldier, a RETRENCHMENT of the attack plans meant he could RETURN to his TRENCH and lay low for a while.

Retrospection (noun): the act of thinking about the past. 2

Think: RETRO-INSPECTION.

RETROSPECTION about the 1980s is a RETRO-INSPECTION that can lead to wearing neon clothes and leg warmers.

Revamp (verb): to revise, improve, or make over. 2

Think: return as a VAMPIRE.

If you're sucked dry by a VAMPIRE, don't worry - you'll die, but then be REVAMPED as a strong, new member of the undead.

Revanche (noun): revenge. 4

Think: REVENGE.

Motivated by REVENGE, the French monarch ordered her general to take REVANCHE on those who had captured the island.

Reverberate (verb): to echo. 2

Think: RE-VIBRATE.

I yodeled in the empty concert hall, and the echoes REVERBERATED and RE-VIBRATED as they bounced off the walls.

Reverent (adjective): having deep respect for. 2

Think: REVEREND.

During church, the REVEREND reminded them to be REVERENT to Jesus.

Revile (verb): to abuse verbally. 2

Think: EVIL, VILE.

My disillusionment with the army began when I tripped, causing the drill sergeant to REVILE me with the most EVIL, VILE insults I've ever heard.

Revulsion (noun): disgust. 2

Think: REVOLT and SHUN.

When the king barfed then ate the barf, I felt such REVULSION that I wanted to REVOLT and SHUN him.

Rhapsodize (verb): to enthusiastically praise. 2

Think: RAPTURE.

The rapper Sisqo felt so much RAPTURE when looking at women wearing thongs that he RHAPSODIZED about them in "The Thong Song".

Rickety (adjective): weak. 2

Think: RICKETS.

RICKETS, a disease that weakens the bones, makes its sufferers RICKETY.

Rift (noun): a break or split. 1

Think: RIPPED.

The RIFT in our friendship was so deep that it felt as though our bond had been RIPPED.

Riposte (noun): a comeback. 3

Think: RIP POST.

After being mocked, the blogger would RIP into his critic's POST with a brutal RIPOSTE.

Risible (adjective): funny; inclined to laugh. 2

Think: get a RISE.

If you like to get a RISE out of people by being a class clown, you're probably RISIBLE.

Risque (adjective): almost improper or indecent. 2

Think: RISKY.

Making a RISQUE joke the first time you meet your girlfriend's parents is RISKY.

Roborant (noun): an invigorating drug. 4

Think: ROBO-ANT.

After I gave him a ROBORANT, my ant felt as strong as a ROBO-ANT.

Robust (adjective): healthy; strong; rich; full. 1

Think: ROBOTS.

Humans wouldn't last long on Mars due to the extreme cold - we sent ROBOTS since they're more ROBUST.

Rotund (adjective): round; full; plump. 1

Think: ROUND TUMMY.

Your pet hippo's TUMMY has grown so ROTUND that it's literally ROUND at this point.

Rudimentary (adjective): basic; primitive. 2

Think: RUDE ELEMENTARY.

RUDE ELEMENTARY school kids are impolite only because their knowledge of social graces is RUDIMENTARY.

Ruffian (noun): a brutal person. 2

Think: ROUGH.

The club hired a RUFFIAN as a bouncer because he was strong enough to be ROUGH with misbehaving drunks.

Ruminate (verb): to carefully reflect on. 2

Think: RAMEN MARINATE.

To RUMINATE means to think about something for at least as long as it takes your Top RAMEN to MARINATE.

Saccharine (adjective): sweet in a fake way. 2

Think: SACCHARIN.

The beauty contestant's personality was so SACCHARINE that there must have been Sweet and Low (SACCHARIN) in her veins.

Sacrosanct (adjective): holy. 2

Think: SACRED SANCTUARY.

The temple was a SACRED SANCTUARY and was declared SACROSANCT to protect it from real estate developers.

Salacious (adjective): appealing to sexual desire. 2

Think: SALIVATE.

All the girls read *Fifty Shades of Gray* because the SALACIOUS details make them SALIVATE.

Salutary (adjective): beneficial. 2

Think: SALUTE.

Sal's cooking has such a SALUTARY effect on me that I SALUTE him.

Sangfroid (noun): coolness and composure. 3

Think: SANG FROG.

"You don't scare me!" SANG the FROG when he saw the fox - he had SANGFROID in spades.

Sanguine (adjective): optimistic. 2

Think: Penguin SANG WIN.

The penguin SANG that he would WIN; he was SANGUINE.

Sap (verb): to weaken. 1

Think: tree SAP.

Cutting your initials into a tree can SAP (verb) its vitality because it will make the SAP (noun) leak out.

Sapid (adjective): flavorful. 2

Think: maple SAP.

We make maple syrup from the SAP of maple trees because their SAP is naturally SAPID.

Sapient (adjective): wise. 2

Think: *Homo SAPIENS*.

Be proud that you're a member of *Homo SAPIENS*; you're more SAPIENT than any other animal on the planet.

Sardonic (adjective): mocking (in a mean way). 2

Think: SARCASTIC SARDINES.

When the seniors saw I ate sardines for lunch every day, they made SARDONIC, SARCASTIC comments.

Sashayed (verb): strutted or walked in a showy or flashy way. 2

Think: Miss America SASH.

Miss America SASHAYED across the stage, showing off her first-place SASH.

Satiated (adjective): satisfied. 2

Think: SAY SHE ATE.

If you SAY SHE ATE, she must be SATIATED.

Scanty (adjective): barely sufficient; minimal. 1

Think: SCANTY PANTY.

Thong underwear is basically just a really SCANTY PANTY.

Scapegoat (noun): one that takes the blame. 2

Think: ESCAPED GOAT.

Even though the dog ate some of the vegetables in the garden, the ESCAPED GOAT became the SCAPEGOAT.

Scathing (adjective): sharply critical. 2

Think: SCYTHE.

Getting killed by the Grim Reaper's sharp, hooked SCYTHE is as about as SCATHING a criticism as one can get.

Schadenfreude (noun): enjoyment from others' troubles. 4

Think: SHADY FREUD.

If your psychologist giggles about your divorce he has SCHADENFREUDE and is a SHADY FREUD.

Schism (noun): a separation into opposing groups; a divide. 2

Think: SCHIZOPHRENIC.

The SCHIZOPHRENIC patient underwent a SCHISM that gave him multiple personalities.

Scintillating (adjective): sparkling; brilliant. 2

Think: SQUINT.

Her sequined shirt was so SCINTILLATING that I had to SQUINT to see it.

Scofflaw (noun): a contemptuous law-breaker. 3

Think: SCOFF at the LAW.

A SCOFFLAW will SCOFF at the LAW he just broke since he has no respect for it.

Scotch (verb): to put a sudden end to; to injure. 3

Think: SCRATCH.

Well, the boss just SCOTCHED our plan to bring our cats to work, so SCRATCH that idea.

Scrupulous (adjective): having integrity, or being exact. 2

Think: SCRAPE the POOP.

If you are SCRUPULOUS, you will SCRAPE your dog's POOP off my lawn.

Scrutinize (verb): to examine carefully. 1

Think: desire to SCREW IN EYES.

I'm an 18-year-old cheerleader - when a dirty old man SCRUTINIZES me, I see the desire to SCREW IN his EYES.

Scurrilous (adjective): obscenely abusive. 3

Think: SCURVY CURSES.

After the pirate developed SCURVY, his CURSES became even more SCURRILOUS.

Scuttle (verb): to destroy; to scrap. 2

Think: IT'S CUT.

SCUTTLE the launch of that Space Shuttle! IT'S CUT from the space program as of 2011.

Semblance (noun): an outward appearance; an image. 2

Think: RESEMBLANCE.

The lie fooled me because it had the SEMBLANCE of honesty, a slight RESEMBLANCE to the truth.

Secretes (verb): forms and gives off. 2

Think: SECRET SEA CREATURE.

The octopus is a SEA CREATURE that stays SECRET when it SECRETES an inky cloud.

Sectarian (adjective): narrow-minded. 2

Think: SECTOR.

SECTARIAN views are shallow because they only consider one SECTOR of the whole issue.

Sedentary (adjective): inactive; lazy. 2

Think: SOFA DENT.

SEDENTARY people make SOFA DENTS because they sit on the cushions for hours at a time.

Sedulous (adjective): careful; hardworking; diligent. 3

Think: SCHEDULE US.

Our SEDULOUS hairstylist is always able to SCHEDULE US since she's so efficient.

Segue (noun): a transition. 2

Think: SEGWAY.

A good way to make sure your friends go along with your conversational SEGUE is to barge in riding a SEGWAY.

Seminal (adjective): important; original. 2

Think: SEMINAR.

If a book is SEMINAL, you're probably gonna have to read it in your freshman year literature SEMINAR.

Sententious (adjective): using quotable or preachy sayings. 3

Think: SENTENCES.

The Reverend Jesse Jackson is SENTENTIOUS because many people quote his SENTENCES.

Sentient (adjective): having sense perception; conscious. 2

Think: SENSED IT.

I knew the alien life form was SENTIENT after I pricked it with a pin and it moved: it SENSED IT.

Sere (adjective): dried; withered. 4

Think: SEAR.

If you SEAR those vegetables on the grill too long they'll become SERE.

Serendipity (noun): luck. 2

Think: SARA ENDED PITY.

After winning the lottery, SARA ENDED her PITY toward herself because of her amazing SERENDIPITY.

Servile (adjective): submissive. 2

Think: SERVANT.

The SERVANT was so SERVILE that he wouldn't make eye contact.

Sequacious (adjective): something that imitates another's idea. 3

Think: SEQUEL.

Your movie is so SEQUACIOUS of mine that it feels like a SEQUEL.

Shard (noun): a broken piece of something fragile. 1

Think: SHARP.

Be careful of the SHARD of glass on the floor; it's really SHARP.

Shelve (verb): to put aside or postpone. 1

Think: SHELF.

I SHLEVED my plan to sabotage my rival and put my notes for it back on the SHELF once I learned I got the promotion.

Simper (verb): to smile in a silly way. 2

Think: SMILE CHIMP.

Have you ever seen a SMILE on a CHIMP? They SIMPER in a way that cracks me up.

Simulacrum (noun): an image or representation of something. 3

Think: SIMULATION.

Coachella audiences saw a SIMULACRUM of Tupac: a hologram that was an incredible SIMULATION of him.

Sinuous (adjective): having many curves. 2

Think: SINE WAVE.

Unsurprisingly, if you graph a SINE wave on your calculator it's going to look SINUOUS.

Skittish (adjective): restless; easily frightened. 2

Think: SKITTLES.

After I ate a 54 oz. bag of SKITTLES by myself, the sugar high made me SKITTISH.

Skulduggery (noun): tricky or sneaky behavior. 3

Think: SKULL HE DUG.

The SKULL he DUG up from the local cemetery proved he was a witch doctor who practiced SKULDUGGERY.

Skulk (verb): to hide or be stealthy. 2

Think: SKUNKS LURK.

SKUNKS LURK and SKULK until it's dark enough for them to eat from your garbage cans.

Slake (verb): to quench or satisfy. 2

Think: LAKE.

If you're a zebra, you probably can't operate a water fountain: SLAKE your thirst at the LAKE.

Slatternly (adjective): untidy or promiscuous. 4

Think: SLUTTY.

If you want to say she's SLUTTY but use a bit more flattery, call her SLATTERNLY.

Slipshod (adjective): careless; sloppy. 2

Think: SLIP SHODDY.

I SLIP when I walk on your SHODDY living room floor because its construction is really SLIPSHOD.

Slothful (adjective): lazy. 1

Think: SLOTH.

My pet SLOTH is too SLOTHFUL to move even when he's really hungry.

Slovenly (adjective): untidy; sloppy.

Think: SLOPPY.

Charlie Brown's friends make fun of Pig-Pen because of his SLOPPY, SLOVENLY appearance.

Sojourn (noun): a temporary stay. 3

Think: JOURNEY.

If you JOURNEY somewhere, it's probably for a SOJOURN unless you bought a one-way ticket.

Solecism (noun): a blunder. 3

Think: SOLE IS IN.

If you put your foot in your mouth - like if you ask a woman her age - it's a SOLECISM - your SOLE IS IN your mouth.

Solicitous (adjective): concerned for. 2

Think: SOLELY LISTENED TO US.

I knew the man was SOLICITOUS because he SOLELY LISTENED TO US.

Solipsistic (adjective): being extremely self-centered. 3

Think: SOLD LIPSTICK.

The model whose image SOLD LIPSTICK became SOLIPSISTIC due to all the compliments she received.

Somnolent (adjective): sleepy. 3

Think: INSOMNIA.

If you have INSOMNIA you're probably SOMNOLENT from lack of sleep.

Sonorous (adjective): having a deep, rich sound. 2

Think: TYRANNO-SONOROUS REX.

TYRANNOSAURUS Rex had a SONOROUS roar that could be heard for miles.

Sophistry (noun): deceptive reasoning. 3

Think: SOPHISTICATED TRICKERY.

Sophocles' SOPHISTRY was so SOPHISTICATED that his TRICKERY made his character Oedipus kill his dad and marry his mom.

Sophomoric (adjective): immature. 2

Think: SOPHOMORE-ONIC.

SOPHOMORES act MORONIC since they're immature and are more SOPHOMORIC than seniors.

Soporific (adjective): causing sleep. 3

Think: SLEEPOVER-IFIC.

That boring movie is perfect for our slumber party - it's SLEEPOVER-IFIC because it's SOPORIFIC.

Sordid (adjective): filthy; foul; morally degraded. 2

Think: SORRY I DID.

If you are a normal person with a conscience and you do something SORDID, you'll be thinking, "SORRY I DID that" before long.

Soupcon (noun): a little bit. 3

Think: SOUP CAN.

After surviving the apocalypse, we only had a SOUPCON of food left: in fact, we only had one Campbell's SOUP CAN.

Sovereign (adjective): independent. 2

Think: REIGN.

If you're SOVEREIGN, you REIGN over your world and no one else does.

Specious (adjective): seeming true but actually false. 2

Think: SUSPICIOUS McLovin.

It's understandable the cashier in Superbad is SUSPICIOUS when she sees Fogell's SPECIOUS license that identifies him as "McLovin".

Spendthrift (noun): someone who spends wastefully. 3

Think: SPEND before THRIFT.

SPENDTHRIFT means someone for whom SPENDING comes before being THRIFTY.

Splenetic (adjective): bad-tempered. 3

Think: SPLEEN anger.

In medieval times, people thought anger came from one's SPLEEN; "SPLENETIC" was coined to describe an angry person.

Spurious (adjective): false. 2

Think: SPUR CURIOUS.

His SPUR of the moment explanation made me CURIOUS if his story was SPURIOUS.

Squalid (adjective): filthy. 2

Think: SQUAT LID.

If the bathroom stall is SQUALID, SQUAT over the LID when you pee.

Squelch (verb): to crush or silence. 2

Think: SQUASH and SQUISH.

SQUELCH the ant uprising! SQUASH them! SQUISH them!

Statuesque (adjective): attractively tall. 3

Think: STATUE ESQUIRE.

I wanted to make a STATUE of the *Esquire* model because she was so STATUESQUE.

Staunch (adjective): firm; true; strong. 2

Think: **STA**y **UNCH**anged.

I'm a STAUNCH supporter of Justin Bieber, so my support for him will STAY UNCHANGED even if he does something really stupid.

Steadfast (adjective): loyal; immovable. 2

Think: STAYED FASTENED.

The fallen soldier's dog was so STEADFAST that it STAYED FASTENED to the ground near his grave.

Stigmas (noun): marks of shame. 2

Think: STICK-MAS instead of Christmas.

One of our STIGMAS growing up was that we celebrated "STICK-MAS" instead of Christmas – we were too poor for any presents but sticks.

Stilted (adjective): overly formal; stiff. 2

Think: STILTS.

The soldier's manner of walking was so STILTED that it looked like his legs were actually wooden STILTS.

Stolid (adjective): unemotional. 2

Think: SOLID.

The STOLID butler was SOLID and expressionless; he never broke down and cried.

Storied (adjective): having an interesting/celebrated history. 2

Think: STORIES.

The most interesting man in the world's STORIED history makes people tell his STORIES.

Stratagem (noun): a clever scheme. 2

Think: STRATEGY GEM.

The general's battlefield STRATEGY was such a GEM that most historians call it a STRATAGEM.

Streamlined (adjective): simplified; modernized. 2

Think: STREAM LINE.

The STREAMLINED shape of a trout lets it swim through even a rushing STREAM in a straight LINE.

Strenuous: (adjective): requiring lots of energy. 1

Think: STRAIN ON US.

The STRENUOUS hike up Mt. Whitney was a STRAIN ON US.

Stricture (noun): a restraint; a criticism. 2

Think: RESTRICT.

The tourniquet around my arm stopped me from bleeding to death, but the STRICTURE RESTRICTED any circulation and they almost had to amputate my limb.

Strident (adjective): harsh; loud. 2

Think: STRIDEX.

STRIDEX commercials are as STRIDENT as the salicylic acid in the pads, in an effort to hold teens' interest.

Stringent (adjective): strict. 2

Think: STRICT GENT.

Our architecture professor is a STRICT GENT: he's so STRINGENT that if your drawing has any eraser marks, he'll dock you a full letter grade.

Stultify (verb): to make ineffective. 3

Think: STUPID DOLT.

If you STULTIFY yourself by punching yourself in the skull, you'll become a STUPID DOLT.

Stupefied (adjective): stunned. 2

Think: STUPID.

Hermione cast the STUPEFY spell on Crabbe, who became so STUPEFIED that he looked STUPID.

Subjective (adjective): personal; unaffected by the outside world. 1

Think: King's SUBJECT.

His majesty considers me to be his SUBJECT and his SUBJECTIVE opinion is that I'm a peasant even though I'm of noble birth.

Sublime (adjective): awesome. 2

Think: The band "SUBLIME".

The band SUBLIME has spawned several cover bands, a good sign that it made SUBLIME music.

Substantiate (verb): to support with proof or evidence. 1

Think: SUBSTANCE.

You won't be able to SUBSTANTIATE your claim that I ate your lunch without evidence that has more SUBSTANCE.

Subversive (adjective): seeking to undermine or disturb. 3

Think: SUBVERSIVE VERSES.

The political poet was detained by government officials for her "SUBVERSIVE VERSES."

Subvert (verb): to weaken or ruin. 2

Think: SUB HURT.

Captain: the torpedo from that SUB HURT our ship and SUBVERTED our morale.

Succor (noun): aid. 2

Think: SUPPER.

If you're starving and stranded in a snowstorm, hopefully your SUCCOR will include some sort of SUPPER.

Succumb (verb): to give in to a superior force. 2

Think: SUCK UNDER.

Do not SUCCUMB to the deadly pull of the quicksand or it will SUCK you UNDER.

Sumptuary (adjective): made to prevent overindulgence. 4

Think: CONSUMPTION-ARY.

CONSUMPTION of harmful things, like cigarettes or alcohol, can be limited with a SUMPTUARY tax.

Supplant (verb): replace. 2

Think: UP PLANT.

After you pull UP a PLANT out of the soil, you should SUPPLANT it with another one to help preserve the environment.

Surmise (verb): to guess. 2

Think: SUMMARIZE.

Since a police report will only SUMMARIZE what happened, one usually has to SURMISE the actual events of a crime.

Surpassing (adjective): really, really great. 2

Think: SUPER PASS.

If you're SUPER at running, you'll PASS everyone due to your SURPASSING speed.

Surreptitious (adjective): sneaky or stealthy. 3

Think: REPTILES.

REPTILES like snakes are good at camouflage because they're SURREPTITIOUS.

Sybarite (noun): one devoted to pleasure. 3

Think: SIT at a BAR.

If you go SIT at a BAR every night to watch sports and drink beer, you might be a SYBARITE.

Sycophant (noun): one who flatters for self gain. 3

Think: SICK OF ELEPHANT.

The animals were SICK of the ELEPHANT because he was a SYCOPHANT who kissed up to the zookeeper.

Synergy (noun): combined action that produces mutually helpful results. 2

Think: 'N SYNC ENERGY.

By forming a boy band and using SYNERGY, 'N SYNC created more ENERGY than they would had they all gone solo.

Synoptic (adjective): giving a summary. 3

Think: SYNOPSIS.

The SYNOPTIC nature of Spark Notes provides a SYNOPSIS of a novel's plot at the expense of the novel's beauty.

Taciturn (adjective): not talkative. 2

Think: TAKES HIS TURN.

If he's passive and TACITURN at the debate and just politely TAKES HIS TURN when speaking, he'll never win.

Tangible (adjective): able to be touched. 1

Think: TANGO-BLE

If you can dance the TANGO with someone – if she's TANGO-BLE – then she's perforce TANGIBLE.

Temerity (noun): recklessness. 3

Think: TEAM ERROR.

If you have TEMERITY, maybe you should join TEAM ERROR because I bet you make a lot of mistakes.

Temperance (noun): moderation. 2

Think: TEMPER ANTS.

At the picnic, I didn't lose my TEMPER over the ANTS, because I possess the quality of TEMPERANCE.

Tempestuous (adjective): stormy. 2

Think: TEMPERS.

Our hot TEMPERS make US have a TEMPESTUOUS relationship.

Temporal (adjective): relating to time. 2

Think: TEMPORARY.

Technically, diamonds aren't forever; in a TEMPORAL sense, they're only TEMPORARY and will turn to dust one day.

Tenable (adjective): able to be defended; workable. 2

Think: TEN ABLE.

The scientist's theory was TENABLE because it was "TEN-ABLE", worthy of being rated a 10 out of 10.

Tendentious (adjective): biased. 3

Think: TENDENCY.

Don't let him judge the beauty contest: he's TENDENTIOUS and has a TENDENCY to vote for the contestants that flirt with him the most.

Tenuous (adjective): lacking substance or strength. 2

Think: TENTATIVE.

At the debate, the TENTATIVE speaker's argument was unsurprisingly judged to be TENUOUS.

Terse (adjective): brief and abrupt. 1

Think: TERSE VERSE.

Haikus are VERSES / That are as TERSE as the lives / Of gentle fruit flies.

Timorous (adjective): fearful. 2

Think: TIMID OF US.

Tim felt TIMID around US since he was TIMOROUS.

Tirade (noun): a long angry speech. 2

Think: TIRED of RAGE.

If someone gives you a TIRADE, you'll probably be TIRED of the RAGE after a few minutes.

Titular (adjective): relating to a title. 4

Think: TITLE.

The TITULAR character in *Harry Potter* is Harry Potter because his name is also the TITLE of the book.

Tonic (noun): something helpful. 2

Think: GIN AND TONIC.

Drinking a gin and TONIC before my speech was a TONIC for my anxiety.

Toothsome (adjective): tasty; appealing. 2

Think: TOOTH SOME.

The food looked so TOOTHSOME that I wanted to give my TOOTH SOME.

Torpid (adjective): sluggish. 3

Think: TAR PIT.

Once I walked into the sticky TAR PIT, my pace became TORPID.

Tortuous (adjective): winding. 2

Think: TORTOISE.

The streets of Boston are so TORTUOUS that you have to drive at TORTOISE'S speed.

Totalitarian (adjective): relating to a government with total power. 2

Think: TOTAL power.

Our TOTALITARIAN dictator uses his TOTAL power to make us eat TOTAL cereal daily - he's a control freak.

Touted (verb): praised publicly. 2

Think: SHOUTED.

Guinness Stout is highly TOUTED; I know this because the guy drinking it next to me SHOUTED its praises in my ear.

Tranquil (adjective): calm. 1

Think: NYQUIL.

Taking NYQUIL before bed made me so TRANQUIL that I slept for 12 hours.

Transitory (adjective): existing only briefly. 1

Think: TRANSIT STORY.

I found romance on the subway, but alas, our love was TRANSITORY: it was a public TRANSIT STORY that only lasted until her stop.

Treacly (adjective): overly sweet or sentimental. 3

Think: TRICKLE-Y tears.

The scene with a homeless puppy is so TREACLY it seems designed to make tears TRICKLE down one's face.

Tremulous (adjective): fearful. 2

Think: TREMBLE.

I felt so TREMULOUS when I saw a shark swim underneath me that I began to TREMBLE.

Trepidation (noun): fear. 3

Think: TRAP.

The haunted house filled me with TREPIDATION; I feared a TRAP would be sprung on me at any moment.

Truculent (adjective): ready to fight. 3

Think: TRUCE YOU LENT.

The armies should write their own peace treaty, because they're still TRUCULENT after that TRUCE YOU LENT them.

Truncated (adjective): shortened. 3

Think: TRUNK ATE.

The elephant's TRUNK ATE so many branches that the tree was TRUNCATED.

Tumid (adjective): swollen. 3

Think: TUMOR-ED.

The cancer patient's large TUMOR caused his abdomen to be TUMID.

Tumultuous (adjective): disorderly; like a riot. 2

Think: TUMBLED US.

The mosh pit was so TUMULTUOUS that it TUMBLED US around like a dryer.

Turbid (adjective): stirred up and made unclear or muddy. 3

Think: TAR BED.

The lake became TURBID when storms disturbed particles from the TAR BED underneath its waters.

Turgid (adjective): swollen. 3

Think: TURKEY IN.

After Thanksgiving dinner, my belly was so TURGID that it looked like I had eaten the whole TURKEY.

Turpitude (noun): vile or immoral behavior. 3

Think: TURD ATTITUDE.

His TURD ATTITUDE made him engage in TURPITUDE.

Ubiquitous (adjective): existing everywhere. 2

Think: YOU BIG QUIDDITCH.

YOU BIG QUIDDITCH fans have made the *Harry Potter* sport UBIQUITOUS on college campuses.

Umbrage (noun): offense; annoyance. 2

Think: UMBRELLA RAGE.

Someone who takes UMBRAGE at his UMBRELLA probably felt RAGE when it broke during a storm.

Unassuming (adjective): modest. 2

Think: UN-ASSUME.

The millionaire's UNASSUMING car definitely didn't make us ASSUME he was wealthy.

Unbridled (adjective): not restrained. 2

Think: UN-BRIDLE.

After I took off my horse's BRIDLE, he became so UNBRIDLED that I had no control over him.

Unconscionable (adjective): unreasonable; not guided by conscience. 2

Think: UN-CONSCIENCE.

It would be UNCONSCIONABLE to leave your two-year-old alone at home - you'd have to have no conscience - an "UN-CONSCIENCE".

Unctuous (adjective): smooth in a fake way. 3

Think: SKUNK-TOUS.

Pepe Le Pew, the smooth-talking, playboy SKUNK, acts UNCTUOUS to charm the ladies.

Undermine (verb): to weaken in a sneaky way. 1

Think: UNDER MINE.

UNDER the ground lay a land MINE designed to UNDERMINE the army's advance.

Understated (adjective): downplayed; made to seem less than it actually is. 1

Think: UNDERSTATEMENT.

"I have no complaints" is an UNDERSTATED way to respond if you're wealthy and asked how much money you make; it's an UNDERSTATEMENT.

Undulate (verb): to move in a smooth, wavelike way. 2

Think: UNDO LACE.

You'll definitely turn your lover on if you UNDO your LACE lingerie while slowly UNDULATING your body.

Uniform (adjective): always the same. 1

Think: Army UNIFORM.

Throughout the U.S., the UNIFORM (noun) that Army soldiers wear is UNIFORM (adjective).

Unkempt (adjective): untidy. 2

Think: UN-KEPT hair.

If you had just KEPT up with your personal hygiene, your hair wouldn't be so UNKEMPT and birds wouldn't have nested in it.

Unruly (adjective): difficult to discipline or manage. 1

Think: UN-RULE-ABLE.

My two-year-old is UNRULY; he is UN-RULE-ABLE and says "No!" to me every time I tell him to do something.

Unsavory (adjective): unpleasant, esp. morally unpleasant. 2

Think: UN-SAVOR.

The icky memory of the UNSAVORY used car salesman was not one I wanted to SAVE or SAVOR.

Untoward (adjective): improper; troublesome. 2

Think: UNDERTOW.

The beach's dangerous UNDERTOW was UNTOWARD, dragging the girl underwater and loosening her bikini.

Unwieldy (adjective): awkward; cumbersome. 2

Think: UNABLE to WIELD.

The ogre dropped his giant club and I picked it up, but it was too UNWIELDY to WIELD against him in battle.

Upbraided (verb): criticized severely. 3

Think: UPSIDE BRAID.

The hippie UPBRAIDED me so much that I was afraid she was going to slap me UPSIDE the head with her giant BRAID.

Urbane (adjective): sophisticated; polite and polished. 2

Think: URBAN.

The farmboy moved to a hip URBAN city and became so URBANE that he threw away his straw hat.

Usurp (verb): to illegally take by force. 2

Think: U SLURP.

I know you're an anteater, but if you USURP my ant farm and U SLURP up my ants, I'll be really angry.

Utilitarian (adjective): useful. 2

Think: UTILIZE.

The military likes to buy UTILITARIAN tools that can be UTILIZED for many different tasks.

Vacuous (adjective): stupid. 2

Think: VACUUM.

The beauty pageant contestant's answer was so VACUOUS that the judges thought her brain had been VACUUMED out of her head.

Vainglorious (adjective): boastful. 3

Think: VAIN.

The evil queen in Snow White is VAINGLORIOUS - because she's VAIN and thinks she's GLORIOUS.

Vapid (adjective): dull; air-headed. 2

Think: VAPOR.

All VAPOR and no substance, MTV is so VAPID that it makes me want to take a nap.

Variegated (adjective): varied. 3

Think: VARIED.

The autumn leaves in Vermont are known for their VARIEGATED colors; last year, they VARIED from red to yellow to orange.

Vaunted (adjective): widely praised. 2

Think: VAULTED well.

The gymnast VAULTED so well that she was VAUNTED by the judges.

Vehement (adjective): strongly emotional. 2

Think: HE MEANT IT.

His warning was so VEHEMENT that we knew HE MEANT IT.

Verbose (adjective): wordy. 2

Think: VERB BOSS.

They call me a VERB BOSS since I am VERBOSE and know a zillion different words.

Verboten (adjective): forbidden. 3

Think: VERB EATIN'.

In North Korea, VERB EATIN' - instead of speaking one's mind - is common since many topics are VERBOTEN.

Verisimilar (adjective): seeming to be true. 3

Think: VERY SIMILAR.

The conman's VERISIMILAR story almost tricked me since it was VERY SIMILAR to the truth.

Vernacular (noun): the way a certain group uses language. 2

Think: VERB KNACK.

Once you develop a KNACK for the way we use VERBS, you'll have become familiar with our VERNACULAR.

Venal (adjective): corrupt or corruptible. 2

Think: VENEREAL disease.

Nuns with VENEREAL disease are, most likely, VENAL: they broke their oaths of chastity.

Vertiginous (adjective): dizzy or producing dizziness. 3

Think: VERTIGO.

Standing on the edge of the skyscraper made me feel really VERTIGINOUS because I have VERTIGO.

Vex (verb): to annoy. 2

Think: HEX.

In *Harry Potter*, casting a HEX, or spell designed to cause pain, on someone will definitely VEX him.

Vicarious (adjective): felt by imagining the experience of another. 2

Think: BI-CURIOUS.

The BI-CURIOUS woman preferred to keep her fantasy VICARIOUS, so she just watched.

Vigilant (adjective): watchful; alert. 1

Think: VIGILANTE.

If you want some street justice, hire a VIGILANTE - they are VIGILANT by nature.

Vilify (verb): to speak ill of. 2

Think: VILLAIN-FY.

The dumpee decided to VILIFY her ex-boyfriend so the other girls would think he was a VILLAIN.

Vindictive (adjective): wanting revenge. 2

Think: VIN DIESEL.

VIN DIESEL often plays VINDICTIVE characters since he has been typecast as a tough guy.

Virtuoso (noun): someone highly skilled at something. 2

Think: VIRTUES (oh so many).

VIRTUES? I have OH SO many, because I'm a gosh-darned VIRTUOSO.

Virulent (adjective): infectious; harmful; hostile. 2

Think: VIRUS.

The swine flu VIRUS is so VIRULENT that it can kill a previously healthy person.

Viscous (adjective): syrupy. 2

Think: STICKS TO US.

The VISCOUS BISQUICK pancake batter STICKS to US.

Vitiate (verb): to impair or degrade. 3

Think: WISH YOU ATE.

If you eat Taco Bell, it will VITIATE your stomach and make you WISH YOU ATE something else.

Vituperated (verb): criticized harshly. 3

Think: VIPER.

He was VITUPERATED so badly that he felt like he had been bitten by a VIPER.

Vivacious (adjective): lively. 2

Think: VIVA LA VIDA.

The Coldplay song "VIVA LA VIDA" means "long live life" and makes me want to be VIVACIOUS.

Vocation (noun): job. 2

Think: afford a VACATION.

If you want to afford a VACATION get a VOCATION.

Vociferous (adjective): loud. 2

Think: VOICE FOR US.

The announcer's loud VOICE, FOR US, was too VOCIFEROUS.

Volition (noun): a conscious choice. 2

Think: VOLUNTEER.

No one forced him to VOLUNTEER for the mission; he did it of his own VOLITION.

Voluminous (adjective): large or numerous. 2

Think: 18 VOLUME diary.

I gave up on reading her diary after realizing how VOLUMINOUS it was - it had 18 VOLUMES!

Voracious (adjective): having a huge appetite. 2

Think: CARNIVORE ATE US.

The CARNIVORE ATE US because of its VORACIOUS appetite.

Waffle (verb): to go back and forth. 2

Think: should I get WAFFLES?

When I go out to brunch, I WAFFLE (verb) between getting WAFFLES (noun) and getting eggs.

Wan (adjective): sick-looking. 2

Think: old OBI-WAN.

In <u>Star Wars</u>, Obi-WAN Kenobi looked WAN even though he was a Jedi master because he was old.

Wanting (adjective): lacking or absent. 2

Think: WANTING a boyfriend.

WANTING (verb) a boyfriend is normal if the romance in your life is WANTING (adjective).

Waspish (adjective): irritable. 2

Think: WASP-ISH.

The trouble with keeping them as pets is that WASPS are almost always WASPISH – they'll sting you if you look at them the wrong way.

Watershed (noun): a turning point. 2

Think: WATERGATE.

Nixon's involvement in the WATERGATE scandal was a WATERSHED for his public opinion and led to his resignation.

Wax (verb): to increase; to grow. 1

Think: Ear WAX.

Thanks to your body's glands, your sticky, orange-brown ear WAX will WAX daily even if you use Q-tips.

Welter (verb): to be in turmoil; to get tossed around. 3

Think: WELTS.

When I surf, I WELTER in the waves and my board hits me; I come out covered in WELTS.

Whet (verb): to sharpen; to make more intense. 2

Think: WET MOUTH.

If you're starving and I show you a picture of a cheeseburger, it will WHET your appetite and your mouth will water and get WET.

Whimsical (adjective): playful; random; fanciful. 1

Think: WHIM.

The princess's WHIMSICAL ideas included her sudden WHIM to travel to Antarctica.

Willful (adjective): stubborn, insistent. 2

Think: WILL-FULL.

The WILLFUL horse was so WILL-FULL that he refused to be trained or ridden.

Wily (adjective): clever; sly. 1

Think: WILE E. COYOTE.

WILE E. Coyote was not quite WILY enough to catch the Roadrunner despite his clever traps.

Winnow (verb): to separate the useful from the not-useful. 2

Think: MINNOWS.

WINNOW the MINNOWS from your catch of fish; they're too small to eat.

Winsome (adjective): charming and pleasing. 2

Think: WIN SOME hearts.

She'll probably WIN SOME hearts at the dance due to her WINSOME manner.

Wistful (adjective): sadly wishing for. 2

Think: WISHFUL.

The "Forever Alone" meme guy feels WISTFUL because he is still alone after weeks of being WISTFUL for a girlfriend.

Wizened (adjective): shrunken and wrinkled, usually due to age. 2

Think: WIZARD.

WIZARDS like Gandalf and Dumbledore are usually WIZENED since they're really old.

Wont (adjective): accustomed. 2

Think: WANT.

It makes sense that you WANT to do things you are WONT to doing, as opposed to trying risky new activities.

Workmanlike (adjective): good but not great. 2

Think: WORKMAN's DESIGN.

A WORKMAN will produce a WORKMANLIKE house design, but hire an architect if you want originality.

Worldly (adjective): not spiritual; sophisticated; experienced. 1

Think: WORLD traveler.

I've been all around the WORLD and I, I, I, I can't find my baby (but I'm WORLDLY now).

Wry (adjective): cleverly and/or ironically humorous. 2

Think: PB&J on RYE.

Surprising me by serving a PB&J sandwich on RYE bread is a good example of my mother's WRY humor.

Zealous (adjective): passionate. 2

Think: JEALOUS.

Zoe was so ZEALOUS about her first boyfriend that she became JEALOUS of every other girl he knew.

Zenith (noun): the highest point. 2

Think: BENEATH.

Once you reach the ZENITH, everything else is BENEATH it.

Zephyr (noun): a gentle breeze. 3

Think: ZEBRA FUR.

The summer evening ZEPHYR was as soft as ZEBRA FUR.

Appendix: Word Roots

*Authors' Note: Word Roots are a helpful way to deduce
the meaning of words that you don't know. They are not,
however, foolproof: the English language is unpredictable,
and full of words of which the standard meaning of the root
is either flipped on its head (for example, the word
"invaluable" means "valuable") or simply inaccurate. In
other cases, the word root could have multiple languages of
origin and thus the meaning of the word is unclear. This is
why mnemonic devices are generally superior to word
roots with regard to recalling the precise definition of a
word. That being said, having incomplete information on a
word is better than having none at all! We suggest that
when creating your own mnemonics, you make sure to take
special note whenever the word root goes against its most
common interpretation.*

A: without.

Think: AMORAL - without morality.

AB: away or apart from.

Think: ABNORMAL - away from being normal.

AC: sharp; biting.

Think: ACID - something that can chemically burn.

AD: toward or near.

Think: ADJACENT - next to.

AG: to do.

Think: AGENT - something that acts.

AL: other.

Think: ALIEN - something foreign.

AM: love.

Think: AMOUR - a love affair.

AMB: to walk.

Think: AMBLE - to walk slowly.

AMBI: both.

Think: AMBIDEXTROUS - able to use both hands.

ANIM: life.

Think: ANIMATE - to give life to.

ANTE: before.

Think: ANTECHAMBER - the entryway before the main room.

ANTHRO: human.

Think: ANTHROPOLOGY - the study of man.

ANTI: against.

Think: ANTIFREEZE - chemical used against freezing.

APT: skill.

Think: APTITUDE - ability.

ARCH: the biggest.

Think: ARCHENEMY - the biggest enemy.

AUTO: self.

Think: AUTONOMY - independence of the self.

BE: to have.

Think: BEFRIEND - to become friends with.

BELL: war.

Think: BELLIGERENT - warlike.

BEN: good.

Think: BENEFIT - an advantage.

BI: two.

Think: BISEXUAL - having both male and female sexuality.

BON: good.

Think: BONUS.

BREV: short.

Think: ABBREVIATE - to shorten.

CAND: to burn.

Think: CANDLE.

CAP: head.

Think: CAPTAIN - a leader.

CARD: heart.

Think: CARDIAC - of the heart.

CARN: flesh.

Think: CARNIVORE - a meat-eating animal.

CHRON: time.

Think: CHRONOLOGY - sequence of events.

CIRCU: around.

Think: CIRCUMFERENCE - the distance around a circle.

CIS: to cut.

Think: SCISSORS.

CLU: close.

Think: CONCLUSION.

CLAIM: to declare or shout.

Think: EXCLAIM - to shout out.

CLI: to lean.

Think: RECLINE - to lean back.

COL: together.

Think: COLLABORATE - to work together.

CON: together.

Think: CONNECT.

CRE: to grow.

Think: INCREASE.

CRED: to believe.

Think: CREDIBILITY - believability.

CRYP: hide.

Think: CRYPTIC - having an unclear or hidden meaning.

CULP: blame.

Think: CULPRIT - one who is guilty.

DE: reversal.

Think: DEFAME - to take away the fame of (through slander).

DEM: people.

Think: DEMOCRACY - rule by the people.

DICT: to say.

Think: DICTION - choice of words.

DIGN: worth.

Think: DIGNITY - worthiness.

DIS: reversal.

Think: DISARM - to take away an ARMAMENT (like a gun).

DAC: to teach.

Think: DIDACTIC - intended to teach.

DOG: belief.

Think: DOGMA - established beliefs.

DOX: opinion.

Think: ORTHODOX - adhering to established opinion.

DOL: suffer.

Think: CONDOLENCES - sympathy for another's suffering.

DON: to give.

Think: DONATE.

DUB: doubt.

Think: DUBIOUS - doubtful.

DUCT: to lead.

Think: orchestra CONDUCTOR.

DUR: hard.

Think: DURABLE.

DYS: faulty or broken.

Think: DYSFUNCTIONAL.

ENNI: year.

Think: CENTENNIAL - a 100th anniversary.

EPI: on.

Think: EPIDERMIS - the layer of the skin on the dermis.

EQU: equal.

Think: EQUAL.

ERR: to wander.

Think: ERROR.

EU: good.

Think: EULOGY - a praising speech.

EX: out

Think: EXCLUDE.

EXTRA: outside of.

Think: EXTRATERRESTRIAL - outside of earth.

FAC: to make.

Think: FACTORY.

FER: to bring.

Think: TRANSFER.

FERV: to burn.

Think: FERVOR - passion.

FID: faith.

Think: FIDELITY - faithfulness.

FIN: end.

Think: FINAL.

FLAM: to burn.

Think: FLAME.

FLEX: to bend.

Think: FLEXIBLE.

FLICT: to hit.

Think: CONFLICT - fighting.

FLU: to flow.

Think: FLUID.

FORE: before.

Think: FORESHADOW - to hint at the future.

FORT: chance.

Think: FORTUNE-teller.

FRAC: to break.

Think: FRACTURE.

FOUND: bottom.

Think: FOUNDATION.

FUS: to pour.

Think: blood TRANSFUSION - transferring blood into someone.

GEN: type.

Think: GENDER - sex.

GN: know.

Think: RECOGNIZE.

GRAND: large.

Think: GRAND Canyon.

GRAT: pleasing.

Think: GRATEFUL.

GRAV: heavy.

Think: GRAVITY.

GREG: group.

Think: CONGREGRATE - to group together.

HES: to stick.

Think: ADHESIVE.

HETERO: different.

Think: HETEROSEXUAL - sexual with a sex different than one's own.

HOM: same.

Think: HOMOSEXUAL - sexual with one's own sex.

HYPER: over.

Think: A HYPERACTIVE little kid.

HYPO: under.

Think: HYPOTHERMIA – body temperature below normal.

IM: not.

Think: IMPOSSIBLE.

IN: not.

Think: INSANE.

INTER: between.

Think: INTERSTATE highway.

INTRA: within.

Think: INTRAVENOUS - within a vein.

JECT: to throw.

Think: EJECT.

JUNCT: to join.

Think: JUNCTION.

LECT: to choose.

Think: ELECT.

LEV: lift.

Think: ELEVATOR.

LOG: speech.

Think: DIALOGUE.

LUM: light.

Think: ILLUMINATE.

MAG: big.

Think: MAGNIFY.

MAL: bad.

Think: MALICIOUS.

MAN: hand.

Think: MANUAL labor.

MIN: small.

Think: MINIMUM.

MIT: to send.

Think: TRANSMIT.

MISC: mixed.

Think: MISCELLANEOUS.

MORPH: shape.

Think: AMORPHOUS - without shape.

MORT: death.

Think: IMMORTAL - without death.

MUT: change.

Think: MUTATE.

NOX: harm.

Think: OBNOXIOUS.

NYM: name.

Think: SYNONYM.

NOV: new.

Think: NOVICE - a beginner.

OMNI: all.

Think: OMNIPOTENT - all powerful.

PAC: peace.

Think: PACIFIER.

PAN: all.

Think: PANORAMIC - taking in all the scenery.

PAR: equal.

Think: DISPARITY - difference.

PARA: next to.

Think: PARALLEL.

PATH: feeling.

Think: EMPATHY.

PED: child.

Think: PEDIATRICIAN - child doctor.

PED: foot.

Think: PEDAL.

PEN: to pay.

Think: COMPENSATION - payment.

PEND: to hang.

Think: PENDULUM.

PERI: around.

Think: PERIMETER.

PET: to strive.

Think: COMPETE.

PHIL: love.

Think: BIBLIOPHILE - one who loves books.

PHONE: sound.

Think: MEGAPHONE.

PLAC: to please.

Think: PLACATE - to calm down or appease.

PLE: to fill.

Think: COMPLETE.

POS: to place.

Think: DEPOSIT.

PORT: to carry.

Think: IMPORT.

POST: after.

Think: POSTHUMOUS - after death.

POV: poor.

Think: POVERTY.

PRE: before.

Think: PREVIEW.

PREHEND: to get.

Think: COMPREHEND.

PRO: a lot.

Think: PROFUSE - large in quantity.

PROB: to test.

Think: PROBE.

PUG: to fight.

Think: PUGILIST - a boxer.

PUNCT: to prick.

Think: PUNCTURE.

QUIS: to search for.

Think: INQUISITIVE - seeking knowledge.

QUI: quiet.

Think: QUIET.

RID: to laugh.

Think: RIDICULE.

ROG: to ask.

Think: INTERROGATE - to question intensely.

SACR: holy.

Think: SACRED.

SCI: to know.

Think: CONSCIOUS.

SCRIBE: to write.

Think: SCRIBBLE.

SE: apart.

Think: SEPARATE.

SEQ: to follow.

Think: SEQUENCE.

SENS: to be aware.

Think: SENSE.

SOL: to loosen.

Think: DISSOLVE.

SPEC: to look.

Think: SPECTATOR.

STA: to be still.

Think: STATIC - still.

SUA: smooth.

Think: SUAVE.

SUB: below.

Think: SUBMARINE.

SUPER: above.

Think: SUPERSONIC - faster than sound.

TAC: silent.

Think: TACIT - understood without words.

TAIN: to hold.

Think: CONTAIN.

TENS: to stretch.

Think: TENSION.

THEO: god.

Think: ATHEIST - without belief in god.

TORT: to twist.

Think: CONTORT - to bend severely.

TRACT: to pull.

Think: ATTRACT.

TRANS: across.

Think: TRANSPORT.

UT: to use.

Think: UTENSIL.

VER: truth.

Think: VERIFY.

VI: life.

Think: VIABLE - able to survive.

VID: to see.

Think: VIDEO.

VOK: to call.

Think: INVOKE - to summon.

VOL: to wish.

Think: VOLUNTARY - of one's own wish.

Index of Words

Abase
Abashed
Abate
Aberration
Abeyance
Abhors
Abject
Abnegate
Abomination
Aboriginal
Abort
Abound
Abridge
Abrogate
Abscission
Absolve
Abstemious
Abstruse
Abysmal
Accede
Acerbic
Acidulous
Acquisitive
Acrimonious
Acumen
Adamant
Adept
Admonished
Adorned
Adroit
Adulation
Adulterate
Aegis

Aesthetic
Affable
Affectation
Aggrandized
Aghast
Algorithm
Alleviate
Altruistic
Amalgamate
Ameliorated
Amenable
Amicable
Amortize
Anachronism
Anathema
Anile
Animosity
Annotation
Anodyne
Anomaly
Antedate
Antediluvian
Antipode
Antithesis
Apace
Apartheid
Aplomb
Apocryphal
Apoplectic
Apothegm
Apotheosis
Appease
Apportion
Apposite
Approbation
Apropos

Arch
Archaic
Arduous
Arid
Arrogate
Articulate
Artifice
Artless
Ascendancy
Ascetic
Ashen
Askew
Asperity
Aspersion
Assail
Assiduous
Assuage
Astute
Audacious
August
Auspicious
Austere
Automaton
Avaricious
Aver
Avuncular
Badger
Banal
Bauble
Beatific
Beatify
Becalm
Bedlam
Beguile
Behemoth
Belied

Belittle
Bellicose
Bemoan
Beneficence
Bereft
Bifurcated
Bilious
Blase
Bloviated
Bludgeon
Bonhomie
Boor
Bootless
Bowdlerize
Bravado
Brazen
Brevity
Brusque
Bucolic
Bugbear
Bumptious
Burgeoning
Buttress
Bygone
Byzantine
Cache
Cacophony
Cadge
Cajole
Calamitous
Callous
Callow
Camaraderie
Capacious
Capitulate
Capricious

Captious
Cardinal
Castigate
Caterwaul
Celerity
Censure
Cerebral
Chagrin
Champion
Chary
Chicanery
Choleric
Churlish
Circuitous
Circumscribed
Circumspect
Circumvents
Clandestine
Clemency
Cloying
Cocksure
Coddle
Coerced
Cognizant
Cohesive
Coin
Commensurate
Commiserate
Companionable
Complicit
Composure
Compunction
Concomitant
Concord
Concupiscence
Condign

Condones
Conflagration
Conflate
Conniving
Connoisseur
Conscientious
Consternation
Contumacious
Conundrum
Conversant
Copious
Cordial
Cordon
Corroborate
Cosmopolitan
Covert
Cowed
Crepuscular
Crestfallen
Cryptic
Culpable
Cumbersome
Cupidity
Curmudgeon
Curtail
Cynosure
Daunt
Dearth
Debauchery
Debilitate
Decadent
Decimate
Declaimed
Decorous
Decrepit
Decried

Defamatory
Defenestrate
Defunct
Delectable
Deleterious
Demagogue
Demarcate
Demotic
Demur
Denigrate
Denizen
Denuded
Deplete
Depredate
Deride
Descry
Desecrate
Desiccated
Despoiled
Despot
Desuetude
Devoid
Dexterity
Diabolical
Diaphanous
Diatribe
Didactic
Diffident
Dilatory
Dilettante
Dint
Discomfit
Disconcert
Discreet
Discrete
Discriminate

Disgruntled
Dismissive
Disparage
Dispatch
Disputatious
Dissemble
Disseminated
Distension
Dither
Diurnal
Divisive
Docile
Doggedness
Doggerel
Dogmatic
Dolorous
Dormant
Dour
Draconian
Droll
Dubious
Dudgeon
Dupe
Duplicitous
Dyspeptic
Ebullient
Eclectic
Effaced
Effete
Efficacious
Effluvium
Effrontery
Effusive
Egalitarian
Egregious
Eldritch

Embellish
Embroiled
Embryonic
Emollient
Emphatic
Encomium
Encompass
Encroaching
Enervating
Enmity
Ennui
Ensorcelled
Entreat
Ephemeral
Equivocal
Eradicate
Eschew
Esoteric
Espouse
Espy
Estimable
Estranged
Ethereal
Etiolated
Euphemism
Eurytopic
Evanescent
Evinced
Exacting
Excoriated
Exculpated
Execrable
Exodus
Exorbitant
Expatriate
Expedient

Exponent
Expunge
Extant
Extenuating
Extirpate
Extol
Fabricate
Facetious
Fallible
Fanatic
Farce
Fastidious
Fatuous
Fawning
Feckless
Fecund
Ferret
Fervor
Festoon
Fetid
Filial
Finagled
Finicky
Fitful
Flagrant
Fleeting
Flippant
Florid
Flotilla
Flotsam
Flounder
Flouted
Flummoxed
Foible
Foment
Forbearance

Foreground
Forestall
Fortitude
Fortuitous
Fracas
Fractious
Fraternize
Frenetic
Froward
Frugal
Fruition
Fudge
Fuliginous
Fulsome
Funereal
Furor
Furtive
Gaffe
Gainsay
Gallant
Gambit
Gambol
Garble
Gargantuan
Garrulous
Gauche
Gaudy
Genial
Germinate
Glacial
Glancing
Glowered
Glut
Gossamer
Grandiloquent
Grandiose

Grandstand
Grasping
Grating
Gravitas
Gregarious
Grisly
Grouse
Grovel
Gumption
Guttural
Hackneyed
Haggard
Halcyon
Hallowed
Hapless
Harangue
Harbinger
Harried
Harrow
Haughty
Headlong
Hector
Hegemony
Heinous
Hermetic
Heterogeneous
Heyday
Hiatus
Hidebound
Hirsute
Histrionic
Holistic
Homespun
Homogeneous
Hubris
Humbuggery

Humdrum
Husbandry
Iconoclast
Idyllic
Idiosyncrasy
Ignominy
Illiberal
Illusory
Imbroglio
Imminent
Immutable
Impassive
Impeccable
Impeded
Imperious
Impetuous
Impinge
Implicit
Importune
Impregnable
Imprimatur
Impromptu
Impugn
Inane
Incandescent
Incensed
Inchoate
Incisive
Incoherent
Incorrigible
Inculcate
Indigenous
Indomitable
Industrious
Ineffable
Ineluctable

Inexorable
Infinitesimal
Ingenious
Ingenuous
Ingratiate
Inimical
Inimitable
Innate
Innocuous
Inordinate
Insinuate
Insipid
Insular
Interloper
Intimate
Intrepid
Inundated
Invidious
Inviolate
Irascible
Jejune
Jingoism
Jocose
Judicious
Juggernaut
Juvenescence
Kindle
Kismet
Kowtow
Lachrymose
Lackadaisical
Laconic
Languid
Largess
Lassitude
Latent

Laudable
Lax
Legerdemain
Levity
Licentious
Lionized
Listless
Logorrhea
Loquacious
Lovelorn
Lucre
Ludicrous
Lugubrious
Lumber
Luminary
Lurid
Macabre
Macerate
Machination
Maelstrom
Magisterial
Magnanimous
Magnate
Malevolent
Malign
Malinger
Malleable
Mandate
Manifold
Marginal
Marshal
Maudlin
Mawkish
Meld
Mellifluous
Melodramatic

Menial
Mendicant
Mephitic
Mercenary
Mercurial
Meretricious
Meshuga
Mettle
Miasma
Microcosm
Milieu
Milquetoast
Mimetic
Minatory
Minion
Misanthrope
Miscreant
Miserly
Misnomer
Mitigate
Modicum
Modish
Monastic
Morass
Mores
Moribund
Morose
Motile
Motley
Mundane
Munificent
Myopic
Myriad
Nadir
Nascent
Nebulous

Neophyte
Nepotism
Nettle
Newfangled
Noisome
Non sequitur
Nondescript
Nonplussed
Nontrivial
Nostalgia
Nostrum
Notorious
Novel
Novitiate
Noxious
Nuance
Nugatory
Obdurate
Obeisance
Obfuscated
Objective
Obstinate
Obstreperous
Occluded
Odious
Officious
Omniscient
Onus
Openhanded
Opine
Opportune
Opprobrium
Ornate
Orthodox
Ossified
Ostentatious

Ostracized
Otiose
Outstrip
Overweening
Pacific
Painstaking
Palatable
Palatial
Palliate
Pallid
Panacea
Pander
Pangs
Paradigm
Paragon
Pariah
Parley
Parochial
Parody
Paroxysm
Parsimonious
Partisan
Pastiche
Pathos
Patois
Paucity
Pedestrian
Peevish
Penchant
Pendulous
Penitent
Penurious
Penury
Peons
Peregrinate
Peremptory

Perennial
Perfidy
Perfunctory
Peripatetic
Permeated
Permutation
Pernicious
Perquisites
Perspicacious
Pertinacious
Perturb
Perverse
Petulant
Philander
Phlegmatic
Physiological
Picaresque
Picayune
Picturesque
Piebald
Piquant
Pith
Pittance
Plaintive
Platitude
Platonic
Plaudits
Plausible
Plebeian
Plenipotentiary
Pluck
Plutocracy
Polarize
Polemic
Politesse
Politic

Ponderous
Poseur
Posit
Pragmatic
Prattle
Precarious
Precocious
Precursor
Predilection
Prescient
Pretext
Prevaricate
Primordial
Pristine
Proclivity
Prodigious
Profane
Profligacy
Profound
Profuse
Progenitors
Prognosticate
Proliferate
Prolific
Prolix
Prominent
Promulgate
Propensity
Prophetic
Propitious
Propriety
Prosaic
Protean
Provincial
Prowess
Proximity

Prudent
Puerile
Pugnacious
Pulchritude
Punctilious
Pungent
Punitive
Pusillanimous
Putrid
Quagmire
Quail
Quash
Querulous
Quiescent
Quintessential
Quixotic
Quizzical
Quotidian
Raconteur
Ragamuffin
Raiment
Rampant
Rancorous
Rankled
Rapacious
Rapturous
Rarefied
Rash
Raucous
Raze
Reap
Recalcitrant
Recant
Recapitulated
Recidivist
Reclusive

Recondite
Recrudescent
Rectitude
Redress
Reductive
Redundant
Refracted
Refractory
Refulgent
Rejuvenated
Relish
Remedial
Remiss
Remunerated
Renowned
Replete
Reprehensible
Reprobate
Repudiate
Repugnant
Requisite
Resigned
Resolute
Respite
Resplendent
Restitution
Restive
Resurgence
Reticent
Retiring
Retrenchment
Retrospection
Revamp
Revanche
Reverberate
Reverent

Revile
Revulsion
Rhapsodize
Rickety
Rift
Riposte
Risible
Risque
Roborant
Robust
Rotund
Rudimentary
Ruffian
Ruminate
Saccharine
Sacrosanct
Salacious
Salutary
Sangfroid
Sanguine
Sap
Sapid
Sapient
Sardonic
Sashayed
Satiated
Scanty
Scapegoat
Scathing
Schadenfreude
Schism
Scintillating
Scofflaw
Scotch
Scrupulous
Scrutinize

Scurrilous
Scuttle
Semblance
Secretes
Sectarian
Sedentary
Sedulous
Segue
Seminal
Sententious
Sentient
Sere
Serendipity
Servile
Sequacious
Shard
Shelve
Simper
Simulacrum
Sinuous
Skittish
Skulduggery
Skulk
Slake
Slatternly
Slipshod
Slothful
Slovenly
Sojourn
Solecism
Solicitous
Solipsistic
Somnolent
Sonorous
Sophistry
Sophomoric

Soporific
Sordid
Soupcon
Sovereign
Specious
Spendthrift
Splenetic
Spurious
Squalid
Squelch
Statuesque
Staunch
Steadfast
Stigmas
Stilted
Stolid
Storied
Stratagem
Streamlined
Strenuous
Stricture
Strident
Stringent
Stultify
Stupefied
Subjective
Sublime
Substantiate
Subversive
Subvert
Succor
Succumb
Sumptuary
Supplant
Surmise
Surpassing

Surreptitious
Sybarite
Sycophant
Synergy
Synoptic
Taciturn
Tangible
Temerity
Temperance
Tempestuous
Temporal
Tenable
Tendentious
Tenuous
Terse
Timorous
Tirade
Titular
Tonic
Toothsome
Torpid
Tortuous
Totalitarian
Touted
Tranquil
Transitory
Treacly
Tremulous
Trepidation
Truculent
Truncated
Tumid
Tumultuous
Turbid
Turgid
Turpitude

Ubiquitous
Umbrage
Unassuming
Unbridled
Unconscionable
Unctuous
Undermine
Understated
Undulate
Uniform
Unkempt
Unruly
Unsavory
Untoward
Unwieldy
Upbraided
Urbane
Usurp
Utilitarian
Vacuous
Vainglorious
Vapid
Variegated
Vaunted
Vehement
Verbose
Verboten
Verisimilar
Vernacular
Venal
Vertiginous
Vex
Vicarious
Vigilant
Vilify
Vindictive

Virtuoso
Virulent
Viscous
Vitiate
Vituperated
Vivacious
Vocation
Vociferous
Volition
Voluminous
Voracious
Waffle
Wan
Wanting
Waspish
Watershed
Wax
Welter
Whet
Whimsical
Willful
Wily
Winnow
Winsome
Wistful
Wizened
Wont
Workmanlike
Worldly
Wry
Zealous
Zenith
Zephyr

Acknowledgments

We mainly used the online version of the Merriam-Webster dictionary (www.m-w.com) for definitions. We'd like to thank Edwin Kotchian for his editing feedback and creative suggestions.

3460563R00174

Made in the USA
San Bernardino, CA
03 August 2013